Gardening
Under Cover

Gardening
Under Cover

A Northwest Guide to
Solar Greenhouses, Cold Frames,
and Cloches

William Head

SASQUATCH BOOKS • SEATTLE

Sasquatch edition copyedited by Don Roberts

Library of Congress Cataloging-in-Publication Data

Head, William, 1946—
    Gardening under cover: a Northwest guide to solar greenhouses, cold frames,
and cloches/written by William Head; edited by Kay Stewart; designed and illustrated by Kate Seigal; construction illustrations by Kristi Waller.
        p. cm.
    Reprint. Originally published: Eugene, OR: Amity Foundation, 1984.
    Includes bibliographical references.
    ISBN 0-912365-23-4: $10.95
    1. Greenhouse gardening. 2. Solar greenhouses. 3. Cloche gardening. 4. Cold-
frames. 5. Greenhouse gardening—Northwest, Pacific. 6. Solar greenhouses—
Northwest, Pacific. 7. Cloche gardening—Northwest, Pacific. 8. Cold-frames—
Northwest, Pacific.
    I. Stewart, Kay. II. Title.
    SB415.H43 1989
    635.9'823—dc20   89-10753
                                                                          CIP

Disclaimer:
This report was prepared as an account of work sponsored by the United States
Government. Neither the United States nor the United States Department of
Energy, nor any of their contractors, subcontractors, or their employees, makes any
warranty, expressed or implied, or assumes any legal responsibility for the ac-
curacy, completeness or usefulness of any information, apparatus, product or process disclosed, or represents that its use would not infringe privately-owned rights.

Other gardening titles from Sasquatch Books
    Growing Vegetables West of the Cascades
    Winter Gardening
    The Year in Bloom
    Three Years in Bloom

Sasquatch Books
1931 Second Avenue
Seattle, WA 98101

Contents

Why Cover Up?

As a gardener in the Pacific Northwest, you are blessed with a mild climate. With very little protection you can extend your gardening season from winter to winter. With shelter from excessive rain, from wind, and from the usually short spells of low temperatures, your garden and greenhouse can be producing flowers and vegetables in those months when you used to look mournfully out the window at wet, dormant earth. You can add months of gardening pleasure at little expense.

Much of the information in *Gardening Under Cover* comes from research conducted at the experimental gardens of the Amity Foundation in Eugene, Oregon, and from extensive surveys of Pacific Northwest cloche, cold frame, and greenhouse users. Many people who had built these useful garden structures were finding that the secrets to successful growing were eluding them. Many wonderful greenhouses were not in use at all; others were being used for storage or to start a few flats of seeds. Cold frames were stacked beside barns; cloches were hosting lush beds of weeds. It became apparent that guidelines and encouragement were needed to help gardeners make use of these tools.

In Europe, gardeners have enjoyed the benefits of using covered garden plots for centuries. Food, herbs, and flowers grown out of season have high value, so commercial growers have had plenty of incentive to master the secrets of gardening under cover. Inventive growers have continually improved techniques and structures. Recently, plastics and recycled materials have expanded the possibilities unbelievably. Today there are dozens of options available at reasonable cost to every gardener.

A plant sheltered by a transparent cover is protected in four major ways:

1. The cover traps heat by the greenhouse effect. What is the greenhouse effect? When a cat lies in a pool of sunlight that is streaming through

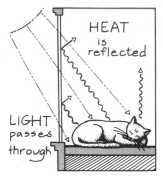

Cats, like plants, enjoy the benefits of the greenhouse effect.

a glass window on a cold but sunny day, a transformation happens to the sun's rays. The visible sunlight has radiant energy that becomes heat energy when it strikes the cat's fur and other surfaces inside the room. Some of this heat is reflected and radiated into the inside air. As heat, it cannot easily pass back through the glass, so inside the window the air warms up. This is called the greenhouse effect.

A covering over a garden bed acts in the same manner. When light strikes the soil and plants, it is converted into heat and it warms the environment within the covered space. This warmth speeds up all life processes, including the growth and development of the garden plants.

2. The cover protects from damaging rain. In the maritime climate of much of the Pacific Northwest, rain is a major culprit of crop failure. Wet conditions encourage diseases that rot stems and leaves of plants and may rot germinating seeds. Heavy rains compact the surface of the soil and can wash seeds out of their shallow soil cover. In very cold weather, wet ground freezes to a depth of several inches.

3. The cover offers frost protection, particularly from late-spring and early-fall frosts. Frosts usually occur after a sunny day during which the soil has been warmed. At night warm air rises and is replaced by freezing air. A covering slows down this air exchange and helps to prevent freezing.

4. The cover provides wind protection. Winds can knock over plants and lower air temperatures dramatically, even on otherwise sunny days.

There are three classes of protective covering for gardening: cold frames, cloches, and greenhouses. A cloche (pronounced klōsh) is a lightweight covering that can easily be moved to different parts of the garden. A cold frame is more rigid and heavy. A greenhouse is a plant covering that is also large enough for people to stand and move in. Greenhouses can extend the living space of a home while at the same time expanding the garden.

One by one, we will explore designing, building, and using these three classes of garden covering. Then you can draw your own conclusions and choose methods that suit your gardening needs.

A garden under cover is protected from the elements and is not damaged by rain, frost, or wind as it would be in the open air.

What Is a Cloche?

The glass bell, or cloche, used by early market gardeners to protect plants.

A cloche is a simple covering which can be moved to different parts of the garden. The word cloche is French for bell. In the 1600s, French market gardeners used a glass jar in the shape of a bell that covered an individual plant to speed its growth. These jars have evolved into waxed paper, plastic, fiberglass, or glass coverings for individual plants, or tunnels that cover entire rows of plants. Most cloches are simple to use and less expensive than a cold frame or greenhouse.

Why use a cloche? Simply because it makes gardening easier. You can:

1. Enjoy more flexibility in choosing planting and harvesting dates. How many times have you set out plants only to see them killed by a frost or to watch them sit without growing until warm weather? How many times have you nursed your tomato plants through summer only to see the fruit destroyed by an early fall frost or rainstorm?

2. Increase the variety of crops you can raise. Many vegetable and ornamental plant varieties that normally would not do well in the Pacific Northwest can be grown successfully under cover.

3. Improve crop quality by accelerating plant growth. Vegetables and flowers should be grown to maturity as soon as possible. Generally,

the quicker a vegetable grows, the better are its chances to resist disease and survive bad weather. Plants grown quickly will be less likely to become stunted and will produce tastier foods and more abundant and lovelier blooms.

4. Reduce insect damage. Early-spring and late-fall plantings can miss the normal cycle of garden pests. We have demonstrated this many times in the gardens at Amity Foundation. Our over-wintering crops rarely have insect damage, because most of the damaging pests are inactive during that period. We stagger our spring plantings of broccoli and cauliflower and find that when we plant later in the spring, the plants are more frequently attacked by aphids, cabbage worms, and root maggots. Midsummer plantings also escape attack by many pests by maturing in late fall or winter.

Cloches are especially well suited for use in the maritime Northwest, where plants need protection from excessive rain and cold winds more than they need protection from very low temperatures.

Unlike cold frames, cloches cast little shade, allowing light to reach a plant from every direction so it does not tend to become spindly and weak. Cloches also have the tremendous practical advantage of being mobile. They are easily moved from place to place. The same set of cloches can be used to cover three, four, and even more crops in the same season.

A cloche can be made of anything that transmits light, so the possibilities for design are nearly limitless. Small cloches can be made of plastic milk jugs with bottoms cut out. Two recycled windows can be leaned together to form a large cloche. A slightly larger cloche can be made using wax paper or plastic circles propped on sticks tall enough

Several small cloches which can be made from recycled or inexpensive materials.

to cover individual plants, with the edges anchored by stones or soil. A wide variety of cloches is available commercially, with an equally wide range in prices. To cover a row of plants or a section of garden, you can build a large cloche or a series of modular cloches that link together.

The general advantages of cloche gardening are:

1. The amount of garden space to be protected can be large or small.

2. The cost of materials can be low.

3. Cloches are easy to build and use.

Some Simple Cloche Designs

Following are three samples of large cloche designs that have worked well for Pacific Northwest gardeners. If you are not experienced at carpentry and wonder how to begin, most of the *Sunset* series on building projects for the home have excellent instructions to assist beginners in woodworking. (You will also find that garden cloche projects are a good place to practice your carpentry skills, because a plant will not mind if a corner is a little crooked.)

These cloche designs are satisfactory from all points of view. They allow easy access to plants for weeding, watering, checking for pests, and harvesting. They will be stable in windy weather, they are easy to vent, can be easily moved, and are reasonably durable, especially if all wooden parts are built with treated or rot-resistant wood or are sealed after being built.

PVC Tunnel Cloche

This cloche is designed to cover a planting bed 5' wide and 19' long. It cost about $45 to build in 1989 prices.

MATERIALS NEEDED		
Quantity	**Unit Size**	**Material**
4	20' lengths	½" PVC pipe
1	20' length	¾" PVC pipe
12	10' lengths	1" × 2" lumber
4	10" lengths	2" × 2" lumber
1	10' × 25' roll	4-mil polyethylene plastic sheeting
1	roll	heavy twine (nylon is good)
¼ lb	4d.	galvanized nails
4		screw eyes

Tools needed: hammer, tape measure, scissors, hacksaw, screwdriver, and handsaw.

1. Cut each 20' length of ½" PVC pipe in half, so you have eight 10' pieces. Cut the ¾" pipe into sixteen 15" pieces. This is easiest to do at the store.

2. Stretch string as a guide along each side of a 5'×19' garden bed. Push the ¾" PVC pieces about 9" into the ground at 34" intervals. If you need to hammer the pipe in, place a board over the top to protect the opening.

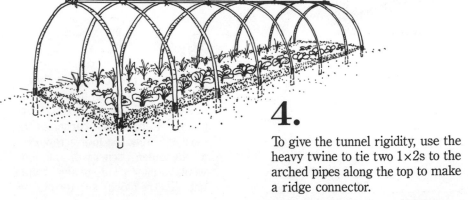

3. Insert one end of a ½" pipe into a ¾" pipe and arch it over the raised bed, anchoring it in the opposite ¾" pipe.

4. To give the tunnel rigidity, use the heavy twine to tie two 1×2s to the arched pipes along the top to make a ridge connector.

5. Center the polyethylene over the tunnel frame. Trim it at ground level. Starting 2½' from each end of the sheet, sandwich the polyethylene between pieces of 10' 1×2s and nail. This gives it weight to hang in place.

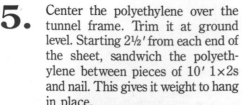

6. Cut the remaining 1×2s into four 5' pieces. Center these to sandwich the plastic on each end.

7. To weed, water, and harvest, lift the wood strip along the bottom and place it on the ridgeline of the cloche. Take care not to tear the plastic.

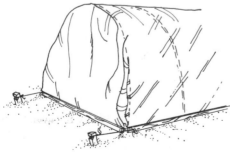

8.

To protect the cloche in heavy winds, make a notch near one end of each of the four 10" 2×2s. Drive a stake 1' from each corner of the cloche. Screw the four screw eyes at the outer corners of the long wood strips. Tie heavy twine between the cloche and the stakes.

Tent Cloche

This cloche is very light, portable, and easy to build. It was designed by Carl Woestendiek of Seattle, and cost around $30 to build. This design covers a 4'×6' area.

Tools needed: saw, screwdriver, measuring tape, staple gun, electric drill with ⅞" spade bit.

MATERIALS NEEDED		
Quantity	**Unit Size**	**Material**
1	8' length	2"× 2" lumber
2	6' lengths	2"× 2" lumber
1	10'× 8' piece	4- or 6-mil polyethylene plastic sheeting
2	10' lengths	¾" PVC pipe
4	¾"× 1"	metal corner braces with screws
1	20' length	duct tape
1	box	⅜" staples

1. Cut the 8' 2×2 into two 4' pieces. Cut the two 6' 2×2s into two 5'9" pieces.

2. Build a 4'×6' rectangular frame, butting the longer pieces between the shorter ones. Secure with corner braces and screws.

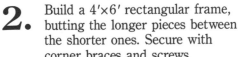

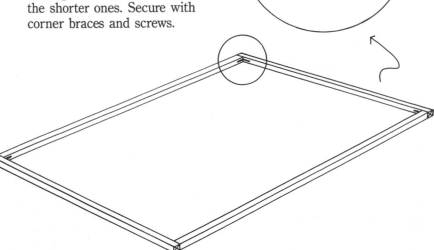

3. Drill a ⅞"-diameter hole, 1¼" deep, ¾" from each end of both 4' lengths. Do not drill all the way through. Leave ¼" of wood at the bottom of the hole for the PVC pipe to rest on.

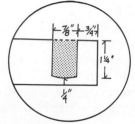

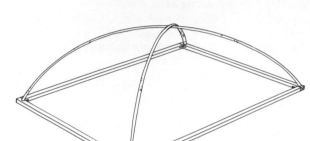

4. Insert an end of PVC pipe into one corner hole, arch it across to the diagonally opposite hole, and insert it. Insert the second piece of pipe, arch it over the first, and insert it in the hole diagonally opposite.

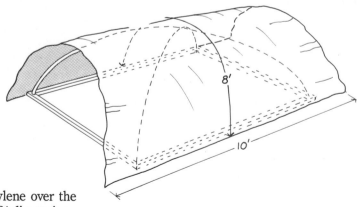

5.

Lay the polyethylene over the frame with the 8' dimension covering the width and the 10' dimension covering the length.

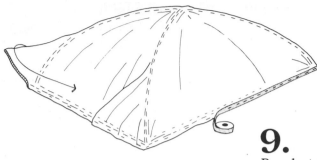

6.

Pull the plastic snug along each 6' side and staple it to the wood at about 1' intervals.

7.

Pull the plastic snug along each 4' side, and staple.

8.

At each corner, fold the excess plastic back against the frame in much the same way as gift-wrapping a box. Staple it in place, leaving the excess plastic hanging down.

9.

Run duct tape around the entire edge of the wooden frame, covering the staples. Then staple all the way around the frame again, this time shooting staples at 6" intervals through the duct tape and plastic. The tape helps to keep the staples from tearing the plastic.

10.

Trim excess plastic from the bottom.

11.

Place the cloche over a garden bed. To water, weed, and harvest, lift the cloche off the bed or tilt up one end. Cut the remaining 6' 2×2 into seven 10" pieces. Drive these stakes into the ground right next to the outside of the frame. This will hold the cloche in place in high winds.

Reinforcing-Wire Cloche

This cloche is another light, easy-to-build design. It demonstrates how a cloche can be made of virtually any materials, if the gardener is creative. This cloche has been very effective in hardening off seedlings. It covers a 5'×10' area.

Tools needed: handsaw, hammer, staple gun, scissors, wire cutters, measuring tape.

MATERIALS NEEDED		
Quantity	**Unit Size**	**Material**
1	5'× 20' piece	6"× 6"-mesh reinforcing wire (used for reinforcing concrete)
3	10' lengths	2"× 2" lumber
4	10" lengths	2"× 2" lumber
1	10'× 18' piece	4- or 6-mil polyethylene plastic sheeting
½ lb		½" fence staples
1	box	⅜" staples
1	30' length	duct tape
4	1"× 2"	metal corner braces with screws
4		screw eyes

1. Cut one 10' 2×2 in half. Cut the reinforcing wire into two 10'×5' sections.

2. Build a 10'×5' rectangular frame with the 2×2s. Secure the corners with braces and screws.

3. Nail the two 5' edges of the 5'×10' reinforcing wire to the inside of the 10' side of the frame with fence staples. Arch the wire over the frame and secure the other edge to the inside of the opposite side with fence staples.

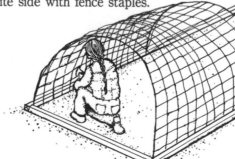

4. Drape the polyethylene over the wire frame, making sure the ends are covered. Using the staple gun, secure the plastic to the outside of the frame at 1' intervals. Start at the corners and alternate sides, stretching the plastic as you go. Folds will have to be made at the ends to give the plastic a snug fit.

5. Run duct tape around the entire edge of the wooden frame. Shoot staples at 6" intervals through the duct tape and plastic.

6. Ventilate by propping up the cloche with pieces of wood, bricks, etc. To prop the cloche open for maintenance, cut a V-notch in one end of a piece of wood and place it so the frame rests in the crotch of the V.

7. Make a notch near one end of each of the four 10" 2×2s. Drive a stake 1' from each corner of the cloche. Screw the four screw eyes at the outer corners of the cloche. Tie twine between the cloche and the stakes to anchor during windy weather.

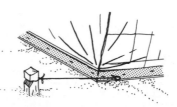

What about Cold Frames?

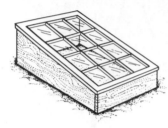

Cold frames fit somewhere between the greenhouse and the cloche in the degree of protection provided. A cold frame has low opaque walls supporting a transparent overhead glazing. Today's cold frames are adaptations of 19th-century coverings called "lights" which were used extensively by English, Dutch, and French market gardeners. The major difference is that the lights were more easily moved to different parts of the garden, while the cold frames of today are semipermanent structures. Usually, one location in the garden is designed for the cold frame.

We have found that in the Willamette Valley a cloche provides enough protection for many plants even through winter. However, we did find cold frames maintained higher temperatures than cloches, so cold frames may be more successful in protecting plants from severe winter cold in other areas. Because a cold frame requires more materials than a cloche, it is usually more expensive and time-consuming to build. It is also less portable.

In Amity's experiment, plants were just as healthy in a cold frame with no insulation, while a reflector hindered plant growth.

Some designs for cold frames include insulation. We did a test at the Amity gardens using three cold frames that differed only in the amount of insulation. One cold frame was uninsulated, one had 1½-inch styrofoam insulation on the inside walls, and

the third had, in addition to wall insulation, a 1½-inch top covering of styrofoam and reflective aluminum foil. This top covering was raised at an angle during the day to reflect extra light into the cold frame and lowered at night to reduce heat loss through the fiberglass lid.

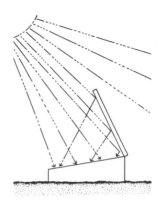

We found the uninsulated cold frame to be cooler than the one with side insulation. However, the plants grown in both were vigorous and healthy. The cold frame with the top insulation performed least well. If we didn't prop the lid open at the crack of dawn, the soil stayed cold and it would take hours to warm up after we arrived and opened up the lid.

The reflector proved to be harmful to plant growth. This is partly because so many days are cloudy in the maritime Northwest and daylight is diffused by the clouds so the reflector prevents light from coming in from half the sky. It worked poorly on clear, sunny days too. The reflected light was so intense that leaves were actually burnt.

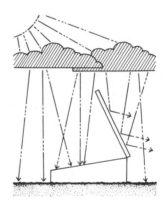

For colder areas of the Northwest, side insulation may be worthwhile. Fortunately, it is easy to add later if it is needed. If you use styrofoam as insulation, paint the exposed surface with white latex paint to protect it from deterioration. White sides also reflect more light to the plants. Top insulation will reduce heat loss even more, but it requires that you open the lid at dawn and close it at sunset. Consider it only if you live in such a cold area that a simpler cold frame will not give good growth.

Many gardeners ask questions about what to use for cold frame and greenhouse glazing materials. A useful comparison of glazing materials is presented in *Low-Cost Passive Solar Greenhouses* by R. Alward and A. Shapiro. Most glazings are similar in light transmission, but vary widely in cost and durability. Polyethylene is cheapest by far, but only good for one to two years. Fiberglass glazing is commonly used because it is a good compromise between low cost and lifespan. Untempered glass is midprice but vulnerable to breakage and best used only on vertical installations or small cold frames. Tempered glass is an excellent glazing material and can frequently be purchased inexpensively as blemished or used patio doors. Every year new glaz-

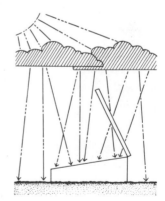

A reflector increases light to a cold frame if winter skies are clear (top), but if they are cloudy, the reflector actually blocks light (center), leaving a translucent lid the best option (bottom).

ing products, such as double-wall acrylics, are introduced, so you should shop and compare before choosing.

Some Simple Cold Frame Designs

We have included plans for two types of cold frames. Both work well in the Pacific Northwest gardens that we surveyed. These frames vary in the amount and height of usable space. Both are easy to build, easy to work in, and easy to vent. Both have hinged lids that can easily be removed in the warm season so plants can grow beyond the confines of the frame.

Four-by-Four Cold Frame

This cold frame is very simple to build and is useful for hardening off seedlings and for growing low crops such as greens, roots, and smaller brassicas. It covers a 4'×4' space. The plans are an adaptation of the cold frame described by J.W. Crockett in *Crockett's Victory Garden*.

Tools needed: hammer, handsaw (or portable power saw), screwdriver, wood chisel, tin snips, paint brush, measuring tape, hand push drill or power drill.

MATERIALS NEEDED		
Quantity	**Unit Size**	**Material**
½	4'× 8' sheet	½" exterior plywood
4	8' lengths	2"× 2" lumber
1	4' length	2"× 2" lumber
2	8' lengths	wigglemold
1	1½"× 8' length	crown molding
1	26"× 8' sheet	clear corrugated fiberglass
2	3"× 3"	loose-pin butt hinges
12	1½" #10 gauge	flathead wood screws
¼ lb	6d.	galvanized nails
¼ lb.	4d.	galvanized nails
½ pt.		carpenter's glue
1 pt.		non-fibered asphalt emulsion
1 qt.		white paint
1	any size	screw hook
8	to fit screw hook	screw eyes
1	6' length	1"× 1" lumber
2	4' lengths	heavy nylon twine

1. Saw the plywood panels for the back, front, and two sides, following the cutting diagram.

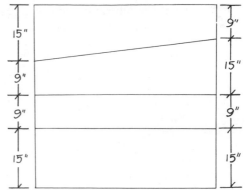

2. Saw the 2"×2" lumber into the following lengths:

number	length
4	48"
4	44"
2	15"
2	9"

3. Center a 44" 2×2 flush with the top edge of each side panel, and nail (6d.), leaving a 2" space at each end of the side panel.

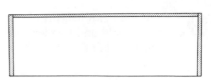

4. Nail (6d.) the two 15" 2×2s to the ends of the back panel. Nail (6d.) a 45" 2×2 horizontal support along the top edge of the back.

5. Nail (6d.) the two 9" 2×2s to the ends of the front panel, and a 45" 2×2 along the top.

6. Make a lid frame of 2×2s, using lap joints. To make a lap joint, mark a line 1½" in from each end of the 2×2. From this line mark down ¾" and draw a line out to the end. With a saw make four crosscuts to the ¾" depth mark. Remove this 1½" part with a wood chisel. Put carpenter's glue along this joint and nail (4d.) the two pieces together.

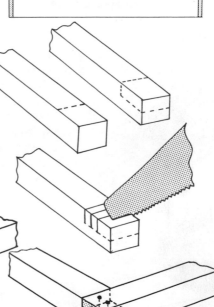

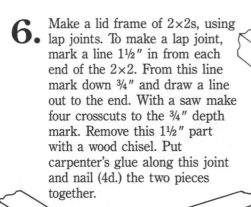

7. Paint the lid frame and cold frame panels white. Paint all wood that will be within 2 or 3 inches of the soil with asphalt emulsion to prevent rot. Asphalt emulsion is non-toxic and works as well as the more expensive wood preservatives.

8. Saw the wigglemold into four 48" lengths and the crown molding into two 45" lengths. With tin snips cut the corrugated fiberglass into two 4' lengths.

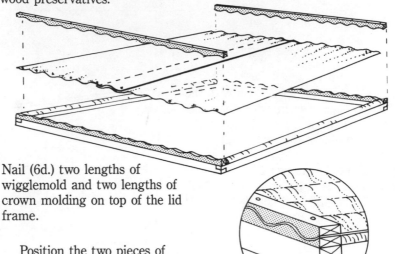

9. Nail (6d.) two lengths of wigglemold and two lengths of crown molding on top of the lid frame.

10. Position the two pieces of fiberglass on the lid frame, overlapping them about 2" at the center.

11. Put the remaining two 4' lengths of wigglemold along the top of the fiberglass so you have a sandwich, and secure with 4d. nails. Predrill the holes to prevent splitting the molding and fiberglass. Use a drill bit a size or two smaller than the nail diameter.

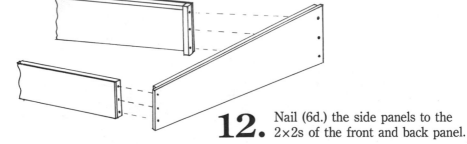

12. Nail (6d.) the side panels to the 2×2s of the front and back panel.

13.

Place the lid on top of the frame and mark the holes for the hinges about 12″ in from each end. Make pilot holes for the screws with a push drill or by hammering a nail in about ¾″ and removing. Secure the hinges with wood screws.

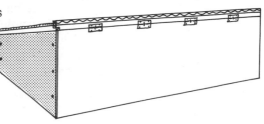

14. Center and screw the hook latch into the front of the lid frame. Screw four eyes into the 6′ 1″×1″ prop pole, spacing them so the lid can be opened at 2- to 3-inch increments for venting and tending. Use the four remaining screw eyes, one at each front corner of the lid, one at each of the two front corners of the base, and tie the two lengths of twine between. This prevents the lid from blowing over the back when it is propped open.

Hermeyer Cold Frame

This cold frame covers a space 4'×8' and is 30" high at the back and 18" high at the front. Its height makes it possible to grow taller crops than in the 4'×4' cold frame. The front is covered with fiberglass to allow more light into the frame. This cold frame was designed by David Hermeyer of Eugene, Oregon.

Tools needed: hammer, handsaw, screwdriver, wood chisel, tin snips, paint brush, measuring tape, drill, power saw (optional).

MATERIALS NEEDED		
Quantity	**Unit Size**	**Material**
1½	4'×8' sheets	½" exterior plywood
8	8' lengths	2"× 2" lumber
8	8' lengths	wigglemold
2	1½"× 8' lengths	crown molding
3	26"× 8' sheets	clear corrugated fiberglass
4	3"× 3"	loose-pin butt hinges
24	1½" #10 gauge	flathead wood screws
½ lb.	6d.	galvanized nails
½ lb.	4d.	galvanized nails
1 qt.		white paint
1 qt.		non-fibered asphalt emulsion
½ pt.		carpenter's glue
1	any size	screw hook
2	4' lengths	heavy nylon twine
8	to fit screw hook	screw eyes
1	6' length	1"× 1" lumber
1	8' length	2"× 4" lumber (optional)

1. Saw the plywood panels for the back and two sides.

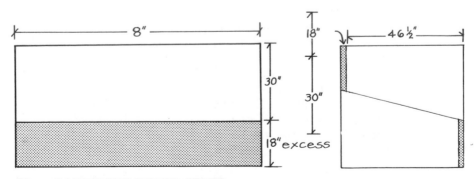

2. Saw the 2"×2" wood into the following lengths:

number	length
5	8'
2	4'
2	44"
2	28"
2	18⅜"

3. Nail (6d.) a 44" 2×2 flush with the top edge of each side panel, leaving a 2" space at each end of the side panel.

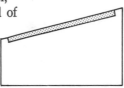

4. Nail (6d.) an 8' 2×2 along the back panel ⅜" from the top inside edge, to permit the lid to close. (An option that will make a better seal, if you have access to a power saw, is to cut an 8' 2×4 lengthwise at an angle of 76° and nail it flush along the top edge of the back panel.)

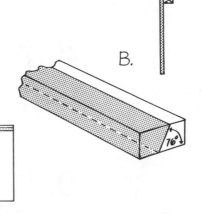

B.

A.

5. Nail (6d.) the two 28" pieces as uprights to the ends of the back panel.

6. Make an 8'×18⅜" front frame out of 2×2s, using lap joints. Make an 8'×4' lid frame out of 2×2s, using lap joints. (Follow the procedure in step 6 of the Four-by-Four Cold Frame instructions for lap joint construction.)

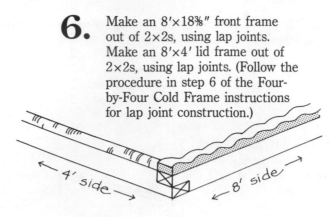

← 4' side →

← 8' side →

7. Nail the 8' length of wigglemold along the top of the lid and front frame.

8. Saw the crown molding into two 45" lengths and two 15⅜" lengths. Nail (6d.) the crown molding to the sides of the lid and front frame.

9. Paint the frames and cold frame panels white, and paint all wood that will be within 2 to 3 inches of the soil with asphalt emulsion to prevent rot.

10. Cut the corrugated fiberglass with tin snips into four 48" lengths and four 18⅜" lengths. Position the fiberglass pieces on the front and lid frames, overlapping them about 2".

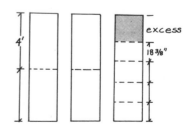

excess

4'

18⅜"

11. Put the remaining four 8' lengths of wigglemold on top of the fiberglass so you have a sandwich, and secure with 4d. nails. Predrill the holes to prevent splitting of the molding and fiberglass. Use a drill bit a size or two smaller than the nail diameter.

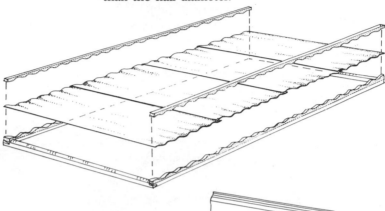

12. Nail (6d.) the side panels to the 2×2s of the front and back. (If you want to be able to dismantle this cold frame, use galvanized bolts and nuts to attach the side panels.)

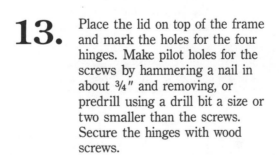

13. Place the lid on top of the frame and mark the holes for the four hinges. Make pilot holes for the screws by hammering a nail in about ¾" and removing, or predrill using a drill bit a size or two smaller than the screws. Secure the hinges with wood screws.

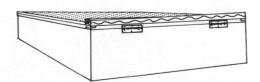

14. Center and screw the hook latch into the front of the lid. Screw four screw eyes into the 1″×1″ prop pole, spacing them so the lid can be opened at 2- to 3-inch increments for venting and tending. Use the remaining four screw eyes, one at each front corner of the lid and one at each of the front corners of the base.

Tie the two lengths of nylon twine between. This will prevent the lid from blowing over backwards.

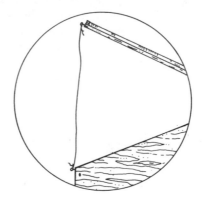

Choosing and Preparing the Site

You should choose the location for your under-cover garden carefully. Think of the amount of gardening you want to do and then consider what type and size of protective covering will suit this need. Then look for the site. The best site is one that is well drained, receives the maximum sunshine possible, has steady, gentle air movement, yet is protected from cold north winds.

Drainage

A gently sloping site is good because it drains easily. Water-logged soil suffocates plant roots, increases the chance for disease, and drains heat from the soil. If your land has poor drainage, you can dig a ditch or lay drain tiles just below the surface, to channel water away from your garden.

Building raised beds also increases drainage significantly. Raised beds and cloche and cold frame gardening go together well, especially in the climate of the maritime Northwest, where a high water table is a major reason for not being able to plant early in the spring. With raised planting beds your soil will drain better, part of the roots will be above the

Raised beds help avoid water-logged roots when the water table is high in winter.

The best garden site: gently sloping with a slatted fence or hedge that reduces the force of wind and lets cold air out.

water table in the warmer environment, and the plants' roots will be healthier. Drier soil actually retains heat better than wet soil, so the benefits are compounded.

There are two popular ways to prepare raised beds. One is the French intensive method and the other is the Chinese raised bed method, recently popularized by Peter Chan's book *Better Vegetable Gardens the Chinese Way*. An effective method developed at Amity, a variation of Peter Chan's technique, follows.

In the location selected for the cold frame or cloche:

1. Strip the grass and sod. This prevents a lot of weed problems later on. Remove the sod 1 to 2 inches deep.

2. Compost the sod in a compost pile by layering it so the grass side of one layer faces the grass side of another layer. This gives ample air space for rapid decomposition. In 6 months to a year the composted sod makes a fine garden amendment.

3. The beds should fit the dimensions of the cloche or cold frame type you have selected. If you have your own design, be sure that the width does not exceed your ability to comfortably reach all areas. With gardening fork or shovel loosen the soil in the beds to a depth of 6 to 12 inches. You don't have to lift and turn the soil, just loosen it.

4. Shovel 3 to 6 inches of soil from the paths between raised beds onto the growing beds. You may want to put bark chips, gravel, or other good walking surface on the paths, so they will not be muddy or sprout weeds.

5. Mix in 1 to 2 inches of compost plus an appropriate amount of fertilizer.

6. Mix thoroughly to a depth of about 12 inches with a shovel or gardening fork.

7. Shape the bed with a rake so the top is flat and the sides slope as the soil permits.

7.

8. Try not to step on the garden beds after they are made. Staying off the beds keeps the soil loose and allows the roots to penetrate easily and the bed to drain quickly.

9. Allow new garden beds to rest for a week or two, as newly combined soil-building ingredients interact and a first crop of weeds may be germinated and turned under or removed. In warm, sunny weather you can place clear plastic on the bed, anchored with stones. The heat trapped beneath this plastic will effectively kill the germinating weed seeds in 1 to 2 weeks. This saves you the labor of hoeing or turning them.

After you've added any amendments, the soil will be ready for you to construct the protective covering you have chosen.

9.

Sun

Your site should receive full sun from 9:00 a.m. to 3:00 p.m. During the colder months, 90 percent of the sun's energy is received between these hours. Since the sun is at a low angle during fall, winter, and early spring, trees and buildings to the east, south, and west may cast shade on your spot. You may need to make a sun chart to find out where shadows will fall. Several books listed in Appendix D give clear explanations about how to make a sun chart, including *Low-Cost Passive Solar Greenhouses* by Alward and Shapiro, *A Solar Greenhouse Guide to the Northwest* by Magee, and *The Passive Solar Energy Book* by Mazria.

For a cloche to receive maximum winter light, the long axis of the structure should be oriented east–west. The difference in light intensity due to orientation is not great during the summer when the sun is high in the sky, but an important difference shows up in the winter when the sun is low.

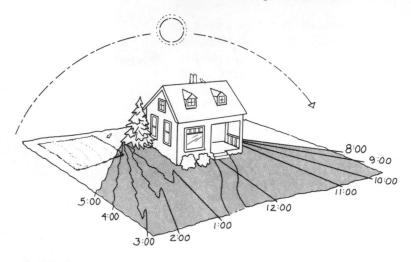

The garden should get full sun from 9:00 a.m. to 3:00 p.m., even in the winter when the sun is lower.

Soil

The spot where you will construct the cloche or cold frame should have good garden soil. The soil in the Pacific Northwest has lots of clay. This type of soil does not drain very quickly and is difficult to prepare for early spring planting, yet is very fertile. Has soil, wet from persistent spring rains kept you from preparing beds for planting even with the threat of frost long past? Clay is probably the culprit.

The experienced Northwest gardener knows that the best way to change clay soil into workable, well-drained loam is to add lots of organic matter. The beginning gardener may want hints on how this is done (see Chapter 13).

Vegetable Varieties and Timetables

Cloches and cold frames are great aids for vegetable gardening. The results of a lettuce-growing experiment at the Amity gardens in the spring of 1982 give an idea of the productivity of gardening under cover. We planted four 90-square-foot raised beds identically with five lettuce varieties on March 2. Two beds were covered with a tunnel cloche and the other two were left unprotected. Each bed contained 200 plants.

The difference between the cloche and the open beds, in both productivity and growing season, exceeded our expectations. The lettuce inside the cloche was ready for first harvest by mid-April, while the lettuce in the open beds was not ready for harvest until mid-May. In addition, the total harvest per square foot was three to four times greater in the cloche than in the open beds.

Consider the economic value of this early crop. If no plants were lost to pests, a grower would have 200 marketable heads of lettuce per bed. Organic red leaf lettuce sold for $.99/head in March '89, in Seattle. By marketing directly, a grower could have grossed $198 for each bed. A tunnel cloche cost only $45.00 to build, which is only one-quarter of this potential yield.

Another example of the benefits of gardening under cover can be illustrated with an experiment Amity conducted in 1981 with tomatoes. We grew five groups of tomatoes. Tomato seeds (Fantastic variety) were started in the Amity greenhouse on March 13. After four weeks, some of the plants were put into cold frames for hardening off before being transplanted to an open garden bed (Group 1) or

Vegetable Seed Sowing Timetable for Cloches and Cold Frames

There are many varieties of vegetables that will produce better, and for a longer time, under cover. The following chart is based on what we at Amity, and other Pacific Northwest gardeners, have found to be successful in this region. Use it as a guide or as a starting point, not as a strict, limiting code. Try other varieties, try other planting dates, and compare them with your neighbors.

A few notes on use of this chart:

1. Vegetables with summer sowing dates will benefit when a covering is put on in cool fall weather.

2. A few people will monitor soil temperatures and plant seed when the soil is within the optimum range given for each type (temperature ranges are taken from *Knott's Handbook for Vegetable Growers*, Lorenz and Maynard). However, by starting seed indoors, where the moderate temperatures comfortable for humans are generally perfect for seed germination, you can start seedlings and transplant later without monitoring outside soil temperatures.

garden bed covered with a tunnel cloche (Group 2). Other tomato plants were raised for six weeks in the greenhouse and transplanted to the cloche (Group 3) or open garden bed (Group 4) without hardening off. The remaining tomatoes were left to mature inside the greenhouse (Group 5).

Tomatoes started and reared in the greenhouse (Group 5) matured the earliest, with ripe fruit ready by July 20. Those transplanted to the cloches (Groups 2 and 3) were ready for first picking 12 days later (August 1) and those transplanted to the open bed (Groups 1 and 4) were not ready for harvest until September 9. We found, to our surprise, that hardening off first in the cold frame did not substantially increase time to first harvest.

If you are now convinced that a cloche or cold frame will expand your gardening horizons, it's time to start thinking of sowing seeds. We want to pass on a few thoughts on sowing seeds in cloches and cold frames.

We have several years of experience growing vegetables under cloches and cold frames. We now start our seed indoors or in a greenhouse in flats and later plant the young starts in cold frames or cloches. We do this, rather than sowing seed directly in the cloche or cold frame, for several reasons. Most seeds require much warmer soil to germinate than they need to grow. We can give them ideal conditions in their tender early stages, when they don't need much space. Later, when the seedlings are carefully transplanted, the garden under cover will provide good growing conditons. You might want to start some seeds indoors and some directly in your cloche or cold frame. You may find some varieties that do as well by direct-seeding, and so can save one step.

Another valuable sowing practice is to plant seeds of a vegetable or flower in a series over 4–8 weeks, at 2-week intervals, in your cloche or cold frame. You'll discover how much earlier and later you may start your garden beyond the dates recommended on the seed packet. Cold frames and cloches give you a buffer period that open-air gardening does not offer. And when open-air gardening begins in the summer, you can wash down your cover and store it in a shady place until it is needed in the fall.

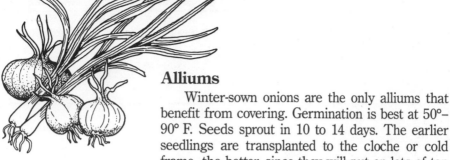

Alliums

Winter-sown onions are the only alliums that benefit from covering. Germination is best at 50°–90° F. Seeds sprout in 10 to 14 days. The earlier seedlings are transplanted to the cloche or cold frame, the better, since they will put on lots of top growth in relatively cool conditions. With more top growth, the onions form a bigger bulb when the weather warms. Onions are light-to-moderate nitrogen feeders.

CROP/VARIETIES	SOW	TRANSPLANT	HARVEST
ONIONS Capable, Early Yellowglobe, Walla Walla Sweet	Jan. – Feb.	4 – 6 weeks	June – Aug.

Brassicas

The brassicas (broccoli, cabbage, cauliflower, kohlrabi, and others) are among the best vegetables to grow under cover, for you can avoid serious pests (root maggots and aphids) by planting out of season. Seed germinates at 50°–85° F in 5 to 10 days. Hot weather and lack of water will cause most brassicas (except summer cabbages) to go to flower. Broccoli can yield long harvests, for after the center head is cut, shoots with smaller heads form; cauliflower, unlike broccoli, does not produce secondary shoots, so you should plant a few seeds every week to produce a longer harvest. Cabbage varieties are available for every season; a frequent reason for crop failure is planting a variety in the wrong season. Kohlrabi is easy to grow, but becomes woody when more than 2 to 3 inches in diameter, so you should plant a few seeds every week to get a long harvest. All these brassicas need extra lime in the soil and are heavy nitrogen feeders. Side-dress regularly throughout their growth period.

CROP/VARIETIES	SOW	TRANSPLANT	HARVEST
BROCCOLI			
Bravo, Emperor, De Cicco, Premium Crop	Jan. – Feb.	5 – 7 weeks	March – June
Bravo, Emperor, De Cicco, Premium Crop Waltham 29, Early Purple Sprouting	July – Sept.	5 – 7 weeks	March – April
CABBAGE			
Golden Acre, Jersey Wakefield	Jan. – Feb.	4 – 6 weeks (or direct-seed)	May – June
April Monarch, Amager Green Storage, Jersey Wakefield	Aug. – Sept.	4 – 6 weeks	March – April
CAULIFLOWER			
Alpha, Snow Crown, Early Snowball	Jan. – Feb.	4 – 5 weeks	May – June
Armado, Pinnacle, Mullion, Snow Jan, Snow Dec, Snow Feb	Aug. – Sept. (June in Wa.)	4 – 5 weeks	March – May
KOHLRABI			
Blue Dannis, Early White Vienna	Feb. – March	4 – 6 weeks	April – May
Lauko, Winner	Aug. – Sept.	4 – 6 weeks	Oct. – Jan.

Cucurbits

This group includes cucumbers, melons, and squash. All require warm soil for the rapid, continuous growth needed to reach maturity. The warm season in the Pacific Northwest is too short to grow most melons, and we must wait until August or September for cukes grown in the open. A warm cloche or cold frame can provide early cucumbers and sweet melons. Melon seeds germinate at 70°–95° F, cukes at 60°–95° F, in 5 to 10 days. Transplant to the cloche or cold frame when all danger of freezing is past (use a max-min thermometer to see how well the covering is working; see Chapter 13). Cut back on watering when melons are ripening. Cucumbers, unlike melons, must be well watered to prevent the cukes from being bitter.

CROP/VARIETIES	SOW	TRANSPLANT	HARVEST
CUCUMBERS Hokkaido, Marketmore, Spacemaster	March–April	4–6 weeks	July–Aug.
MELON (Cantaloupe) Harper, Hybrid Oregon Delicious, Sweet Granite. Almost any exotic variety.	March–April	4–6 weeks	Aug.–Sept.
MELON (Watermelon) Sugar Baby, Garden Baby (too big for most frames)	March–April	4–6 weeks	Aug.–Sept.

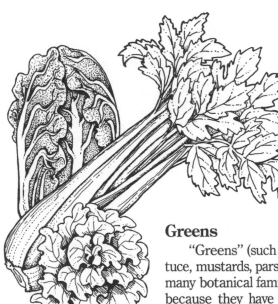

Greens

"Greens" (such as Chinese cabbage, celery, lettuce, mustards, parsley, and spinach) are plants from many botanical families. They are grouped together because they have similar requirements and your desire to balance the use of the cold frame or cloche may mean selecting a few greens, a few roots, etc. Some greens such as chard, collards, endive, and kale are very hardy and can grow into and through most winters without protection. Most other greens will benefit with the modest protection of a cloche or cold frame.

Chinese cabbage, lettuce, mustard greens, and spinach germinate at about 45°–75° F and celery at 50°–85° F, with the time for germination ranging widely among the different greens. To grow greens fast, for best flavor, be sure to side-dress regularly with nitrogen.

CROP/VARIETIES	SOW	TRANSPLANT	HARVEST
CHINESE CABBAGE (Brassica, used as a Green) Spring A-1, Takii	Feb. – March	4 – 6 weeks	May – June
CELERY Utah 52-70 Improved, Green Giant, Golden Self-Blanching	Feb. – March	6 – 8 weeks	July – Oct.
LETTUCE (Head) Ithaca	Feb. – March	4 – 6 weeks (or direct-seed)	May – June
Arctic King	Aug. – Sept.	4 – 6 weeks (or direct-seed)	Oct. – Dec.
LETTUCE (Looseleaf) Black Seeded Simpson, Salad Bowl, Buttercrunch, Merveille, Cosmo MC, Oak Leaf, Romaine, Prizehead	Jan. – March	4 – 6 weeks (or direct-seed)	April – June
All Year Round, Trocadero, Winter Marvel, Winter Density	Aug. – Sept.	4 – 6 weeks	Oct. – April
MUSTARD GREENS Chinese Pac Choi, Green Wave, Tai Sai, Tendergreen, Spring Raab, Watercress	Jan. – March	3 – 5 weeks	March – May
Chinese Pac Choi, Green Wave, Kyona (Mizuna), Spring Raab, Tai Sai	Sept. – Oct.	3 – 5 weeks	Nov. – March
PARSLEY Green Velvet, Plain Leaf, Delikat	Jan. – Feb.	4 – 6 weeks	April – Oct.
Green Velvet, Plain Leaf, Delikat	July – Aug.	4 – 6 weeks	Oct. – April
SPINACH Longstanding Blooms- dale, Indian Summer	Jan. – Feb.	3 – 5 weeks (or direct-seed)	March – May
Winter Bloomsdale, Indian Summer	Sept. – Oct.	3 – 5 weeks	Feb. – March

Root Crops

Root crops benefit by being grown out of season under cover, thus avoiding infestation by root maggots. Beets, carrots, and radishes will germinate at 45°–85° F. Radishes sprout in 1 week, beets in 1 to 2 weeks, while carrots may take 3 weeks. We have had good luck with transplanting seedlings of all root crops. All root crops, especially carrots, grow best in loose, crumbly soil. They all need lots of potassium and phosphorus for fast root growth, so add phosphorus in the form of bone meal when transplanting. Stagger plantings so you have continuous supplies of all.

CROP/VARIETIES	SOW	TRANSPLANT	HARVEST
BEET Detroit Dark Red, Early Wonder, "Boltardy" tends to bolt.	Jan.–March	4–6 weeks (or direct-seed)	March–June
Lutz, Winterkeeper, Little Ball	Aug.–Sept.	4–6 weeks	Oct.–Dec.
CARROT Kinko, Nantes, Amsterdam Forcing	Jan.–Feb.	5–6 weeks (or direct-seed)	April–June
Caramba, Kinko, Nantes, Scarlet Keeper	Aug.–Sept.	5–6 weeks (or direct-seed)	Nov.–Feb.
RADISH Champion, Marabelle	Jan.–April	2–3 weeks (or direct-seed)	Feb.–June
Champion, Marabelle	Sept.–Oct.	2–3 weeks (or direct-seed)	Oct.–Jan.

Solanaceae

The Solanaceae include eggplants, peppers, and tomatoes. All, especially eggplants and peppers, grow slowly in cool weather and are severely and permanently stunted if temperatures fall below 45° F. They are ideal for cloche and cold frame after the danger of low temperatures is past. Eggplants germinate at 75°–95° F, peppers at 65°–95° F, and tomatoes at 60°–85° F in 1 to 2 weeks. We have put tomatoes in a tunnel cloche in early April, kept them covered through June, and harvested in July! All Solanaceae require a slightly acid soil with abundant phosphorus and magnesium. Side-dress with compost and bone meal 4 weeks after transplanting and again when first fruit appears.

CROP/VARIETIES	SOW	TRANSPLANT	HARVEST
EGGPLANT Black Beauty, Dusky, Early Black Egg	March–April	6–8 weeks	July–Aug.
PEPPERS Any	March–April	6–8 weeks	July–Sept.
TOMATOES Early Swedish, Sprinter, Sub-Arctic, Willamette	March–April	6–8 weeks	July–Sept.

Successful Techniques for Cloche and Cold Frame Gardening

Each time you try a new gardening method, you master it partly by trial and error. It's fun, but it's frustrating, too. This will be true when you use a cloche or cold frame. Our experience at the Amity gardens, though, can help you sidestep some potential problems and use techniques which we have used to produce bountiful harvests.

When you garden under cloches and cold frames, you need to pay special attention to temperature, humidity, and soil moisture. In addition, we recommend following the same good garden practices that make open-air gardening succeed: know your plants' special needs, prevent disease and pest problems, prepare soil well, and apply fertilizer as needed. (These general practices will be discussed briefly in Chapters 13 and 14.)

Opening the ends of the tunnel cloche creates a breeze as warm air leaves.

Venting

When in doubt, vent. Except during long freezing periods, get into the habit of opening your cold frame or cloche during the day and closing it at night. Venting is needed to control temperature and humidity, and to provide a change of air for the plants, all of which helps prevent outbreaks of mold and other diseases.

Prop a cold frame lid open using a pole with adjustable opening hooks (as described in Chapter 2). On overcast days the lid only has to be propped open a few inches. On sunny days, opening the lid a foot or two is sufficient. When the weather becomes warm, take the lid off the cold frame.

In general, the same guidelines apply to cloches as to cold frames: it is always safer to vent. Most of our experience has been with the tunnel cloche, which is very easy to vent. On cloudy days we open the end away from the wind. On sunny days we open both ends. A breeze is created by the warm air leaving the cloche. As spring progresses we leave one end open continuously, and when the weather gets hot the plastic is taken off. If weather gets cold again, the plastic can easily be put back on.

Watering

Generally, the more you vent, the more you will have to water. Venting allows moist air to escape, and the movement of air through a cold frame or cloche can quickly dry out soil.

When a cold frame or cloche is closed, moisture that would escape to the air condenses on the glazing and returns back to the soil. During damp and cloudy periods you may not have to water for weeks at a time.

The easiest way to determine if your plants need water is to dig down 4 to 6 inches into your bed. If the soil is dry to that depth, your plants need water. Also watch your plants: if they begin to wilt, they need water.

Light, frequent watering is useful during seed germination and immediately after transplanting, but after the seedlings are established, deep and thorough watering is needed. A light once-over does more harm than good. Unless the soil is wet to the level of the deeper roots, the shallow roots will develop at the expense of the deeper ones. Because the surface dries out faster than the deeper soil, shallow watering creates a vicious cycle in which more-frequent watering is needed to keep the plants from wilting. Deeper watering also allows you to plant closer together, because the roots will go down instead of spreading sideways.

As a general rule, you need to water so that the soil is wet to a depth of 4 to 6 inches. The length of time this will take depends on the delivery rate of the system you use and the rate the soil absorbs it. You need to decide how long to water by observing your own system.

The best time to water is in the morning. Plants will be doing most of their growing during the day and need the water for photosynthesis. Watering in the morning also allows the plants to dry out by evening, which reduces the chance of mildew and rot.

Your choice of watering techniques should fit the needs of the plants and the amount of time you want

A watering wand (left) extends your reach, while a canvas soaker hose (below) winds easily around plants.

to spend in the garden. Hand-watering is good for starts and other plants in containers, but it takes some time to thoroughly deep-water mature crops by hand. A nice garden tool for hand-watering is a watering wand. With the long handle, you can reach individual plants at soil level and at the back of the cold frame. You can get nozzles which will provide different sprays.

An ideal way to water under a cloche is with a soaker hose. We have found that a canvas soaker hose works very well and is easy to wind around plants. Inexpensive timers can be purchased that shut the water off automatically and do not require electricity. Electric timers also can be purchased to turn the water on or off at preset times.

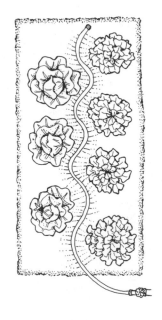

Drip irrigation is ideally suited for raised-bed cloche gardening. In a drip system, small plastic tube "emitters" about ⅛ inch in diameter are inserted into a larger tube and spaced so the bed is watered evenly. The spacing varies depending on the delivery rate of the system. Water is applied slowly to the plants to completely saturate the root zone. This eliminates waste due to surface runoff, puddling, and evaporation.

If you live in a water-short area, or if you are concerned about water conservation, drip systems are a proven success. You can find out about them through magazines, stores, and catalogs. The simplest drip system will cost about $80 to cover 500 square feet. If you want to automate it, the cost more than doubles.

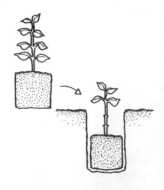

Hardening Off

If you are going to transplant starts from inside to the open garden, harden off plants in a cold frame or cloche first. Hardening off involves reducing watering and leaving the starts under cover for one to two weeks. This gives the plants more resistance to sudden temperature shifts. We found that plants that are transplanted to be grown in a cloche or cold frame do not need to be hardened off.

Transplanting to the Cloche or Cold Frame

Young plants transplanted to a garden under cover require the same care as those transplanted to the open garden. We find it helpful to give transplants a boost by mixing 1 gallon of compost and 1 cup of bone meal, and putting a handful of this mix in the bottom of the transplant hole to enhance rapid growth.

Plant upright plants, such as broccoli, tomato, pepper, or eggplant, deep enough to cover some stem, after pinching off the leaves on the stem section that will be buried. Plants that grow from the crown, such as parsley, beets, chard, onions, or cabbage, should be planted so the ground level is the same before and after transplanting.

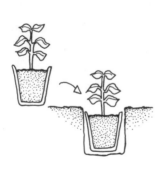

Peat pots can be placed directly in the soil, but it is useful to score the sides with a knife so the plant can break out more easily. Be sure to plant peat pots deep enough to cover the upper edges with soil. If you do not, the exposed edge acts as a wick and robs water from the plant's roots.

It is best to transplant on an overcast day (which should not be too hard to find in the maritime Northwest) or near evening. Right after transplanting, the seedlings may wilt. Be sure to give them plenty of water and protect them from strong winds and full sun for a week or so. You may need to attach a screen or white cloth over the cold frame or cold frame glazing to shade the plants during the first week.

Transplanting depths for upright plants, plants that grow from the crown, and plants in peat pots.

Later in the spring when the soil warms up, you can bypass transplanting and sow seed directly under cover. Keep the soil moist, and thin seedlings to give each one room for full development. Carefully thinned plants, with good root systems, can be transplanted to other areas.

Crop Rotation

As time goes on and you have grown a series of crops under your cloche or cold frame, you should pay attention to the influences that each crop has on the succeeding ones and upon the soil. Rotating the crops you grow in a garden bed will help keep your soil rich and free of disease. Try *not* to raise vegetables from the same group successively in the same space. Each group member has similar nutrient requirements and falls prey to similar insect and disease problems. If possible, arrange your planting every year so different kinds of plants take turns in each part of the garden bed. With a cloche, you may grow under cover in various parts of a large garden. Rest each bed every two or three years by growing green manure crops in it.

Crimson clover

Green Manuring

You will need to add lots of organic material to soil in a cloche or cold frame if you want to support a year-round garden. Your household garbage, leaves, and grass may not supply enough organic matter, and hauling in manure and other organic goodies may not be possible. What are you to do?

You can start growing green manure cover crops. A green manure crop is grown simply to be tilled back into the soil or used in compost. Another common name for this practice is cover cropping. Green manuring does a lot of good things:

1. Covers the soil and prevents erosion and compaction caused by persistent rains.

2. Ties up nutrients in its roots and leaves that would otherwise be washed out of the soil.

3. Keeps weeds down by crowding and shading them out.

4. Adds organic matter and helps improve the soil by creating a porous network of roots.

Legumes can be particularly useful as a cover crop because they add nitrogen to the soil, although they also require special sowing practices as well as higher soil fertility.

A green manure crop needs to grow quickly to protect the soil and to shade any weeds. Late-fall and early-spring plantings may be slow to germinate and grow because of low temperatures. Putting a cloche over your cover crop will reduce germination time and increase growth rate.

When planting time approaches, cut the cover crop and spade it into the soil. If the cover crop has put on a lot of growth, the tops can first be cut off and composted either in the bed or in a compost pile. Cut the crop before it has gone to seed, because stalks become too woody to decompose, and seed may sprout and compete with the vegetable crops.

Wet soil could prevent you from turning a green manure crop under in early spring. Covering the planting bed with a cloche will dry the soil out quickly, enabling you to easily turn the cover crop.

Green Manure Crops for the Pacific Northwest

The two sowing periods are for winter green manuring or for summer green manuring. The soil cools rapidly in October, so fall sowings should be made as early as possible or the crop should be covered.

Crop	Amount per 100 Sq. Ft.	When to Sow	Comments
ANNUAL RYEGRASS	¼ pound	Sept.–Oct.	1. Be sure to get annual, not perennial. 2. Mixes well with legumes.
AUSTRIAN FIELD PEAS	1–2 pounds	Sept.–mid-Oct. Feb.–April	1. Does not require as rich a soil as Crimson Clover. 2. Very cold-hardy. 3. Adds nitrogen to the soil.
BUCKWHEAT	¼ pound	Sept.–Oct. April–June	1. Stems are hollow and easy to till by hand. 2. Does not overwinter well.
CRIMSON CLOVER	¼ pound	Sept.–Oct. Feb.–April	1. Likes well-limed and well-drained soil. 2. Delicate roots are easy to spade up by hand. 3. Adds nitrogen to the soil. 4. Requires higher soil fertility to do well.
CORN SALAD	1–2 ounces	Sept.–Oct. Feb.–April	1. Edible green. 2. Dense root system harder to turn under. 3. Self-seeding. 4. Touchy, germination a problem.
FAVA BEANS	1–2 pounds	Sept.–Oct. Feb.–March	1. May not survive cold winters. 2. Adds nitrogen to the soil. 3. Look for new hardy varieties. 4. Provides edible crop.
TYFON	1 ounce	Sept.–Oct. April–July	1. Edible green. 2. Very cold-hardy. 3. Good for late-summer cover crops.

Designing for More than a Cover

A cloche or cold frame is plant-sized, but a green-house is large enough for people to work in, walk through, and even dine or relax in. Because a green-house is so much larger, it needs more heat to provide a good growing environment for plants or a comfort level for the people using it. In years past, the cost of heating conventional greenhouses discouraged many people from using them. Solar greenhouses are cheaper to heat because they are designed to effectively capture the sun's rays and to reduce heat loss.

Three design features distinguish a solar green-house from a conventional one:

1. The glazed surface faces south to capture the low-angle winter sun.

2. Areas not receiving direct winter sun are solid and well insulated to minimize heat loss.

3. Excess solar energy is stored in massive objects like rock, earth, and water to be later released to the greenhouse at night and during cloudy periods.

These design features influence the location and shape of the greenhouse, the amount of space available for growing and living areas, which areas are best for plants, and what type of equipment is needed to manipulate the greenhouse environment.

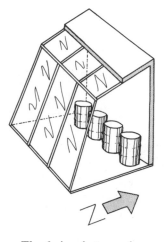

The design features of a solar greenhouse: glazing that faces south, insulation to the north, and some form of heat storage.

Deciding on Greenhouse Use

Many people think of a solar greenhouse as a tool that can add heat to a home or food to a pantry. A greenhouse becomes much more when it becomes a place used in the daily routines of eating, relaxing, and working.

In 1982, Amity conducted a survey of over 100 solar greenhouses in western Oregon and Washington in order to see how people were using them and what useful growing information they had. About 90 greenhouses were attached to homes, while the remainder were freestanding units used by schools, community groups, or commercial growers. To our surprise, a quarter of them were empty, and almost half had very little use. In many cases, people were putting in so much heat storage that they were crowding themselves out. Some people lacked horticultural guidelines to use the greenhouse productively.

The attached greenhouses that were used the most had part of the greenhouse designed as a living space. For example, one owner had divided the greenhouse by a wall and door, using one third as a plant nursery while integrating the rest into the home with plants, chairs, tables, and plenty of space for people to enjoy the green, warm environment.

Design features that emphasize usefulness and comfort contribute to the success of these lived-in solar greenhouses. Many books discuss design and construction of solar greenhouses, so you can build a durable and sound structure. The fact is, though, that your primary concerns should be to design for a fully *enjoyable* and *useful* greenhouse. These are the factors we will look at in detail in this chapter.

Choosing the Site for the Greenhouse

For best solar heat collection, greenhouses should be oriented so the glazing faces as near to true south (not magnetic south) as possible. Don't worry if circumstances won't allow for this ideal orientation. Orientations off as much as 45° from true south receive only 20 percent less solar radiation.

Note obstructions to the low winter sun, such as hills, trees, and other buildings. A sun chart (see Chapter 3) will show how these features influence your site. If possible, site the greenhouse so it is sheltered from prevailing cold winds. Note winter cloud patterns; if mornings are clear and afternoons are cloudy, orient the greenhouse more to the east to capture the morning sun.

All these factors affect your decision about the building site. They should also influence the decision to make either a freestanding or attached greenhouse. Spend some time at your site and get to know the local weather and the sun's pattern before building.

Your greenhouse should be designed with people in mind as well as plants.

Choosing the Shape of the Greenhouse

The angle of the south-facing glazing strongly influences the usefulness of a greenhouse. For best heat collection, the glazing angle should be determined by adding 15° to the latitude. Using this formula, the glazing angle would be 60° above horizontal in Portland, which is at 45° latitude. However, as the glazing is tilted more toward horizontal there is less usable greenhouse space. The following tables show that use characteristics differ among various shapes of freestanding and attached greenhouses.

Relation of Greenhouse Shape to Greenhouse Function
Adapted from P. Chapel, *The City Greenhouse Book.*

ATTACHED GREENHOUSE SHAPE						
WINTER OPERATION	Good (fall and spring shading)	Very good	Very good	Excellent	Excellent	Good (moderate heat loss)
SUMMER OPERATION	Poor for plants (excellent for shading)	Good	Good	Fair (may overheat)	Good	Fair (may overheat)
CONSTRUCTION COST	Medium	Medium	Low	Low	Low	Low
HEATING COST	Medium (some shading)	Low	Low	Low	Low	Medium (some heat loss)
USER ACCESSIBILITY	Excellent (vertical walls)	Very Good	Good	Good	Poor (sloping walls)	Poor (sloping walls)
PLANTING AREA	Small	Large	Large	Large	Small	Small
FREESTANDING GREENHOUSE SHAPE						
WINTER OPERATION	Good (fall and spring shading)	Good	Good	Excellent	Excellent	Good (moderate heat loss)
SUMMER OPERATION	Fair (north-side shading)	Good	Good	Very Good	Very Good	Fair (may overheat)
CONSTRUCTION COST	Medium	Medium	Medium	Medium	Low	Low
HEATING COST	Medium (some heat loss)	Low	Low	Low	Low	Medium (some heat loss)
USER ACCESSIBILITY	Excellent (vertical walls)	Excellent (vertical walls)	Very good	Very good	Very good	Fair (sloping walls)
PLANTING AREA	Medium (some shading)	Large	Large	Large	Medium (sloping walls)	Small (sloping walls)

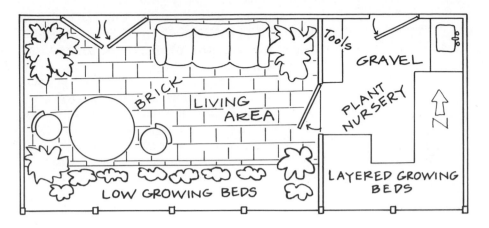

Making a Productive and Livable Space

When you are ready to design the interior of the greenhouse, spend time planning it first on paper. You can figure out where to fit heat storage, walks, plant beds, tool storage, sink and work space, and living space. You can experiment with different furnishings for dining, reading, or viewing. You can try schemes that use the vertical space for hanging baskets, trellises, and tall plants. You can plan for ease of watering and good air circulation.

As you plan, you will find how much variety you can create in a solar greenhouse. If your plan is fun and functional, the greenhouse will be an enduring part of your life.

Above, an attached greenhouse with "living space" emphasis. Below, the same greenhouse designed with "growing space" emphasis.

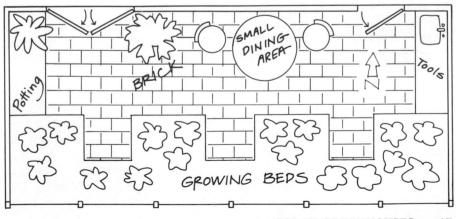

Start out with a floor plan. This is a bird's-eye view of the greenhouse. It shows heat storage, living space, walkways, planting beds, benches, and workspace.

Heat storage. Each plant grows best in a particular heat range. Some prefer cool temperatures, 45° to 65° F, while others need warmth in the 65° to 85° F range. You can regulate the heat range in a solar greenhouse to satisfy the needs of your plants. For example, even in the winter the sun can heat the greenhouse more than is needed. This excess heat can be absorbed and stored by rock, earth, or water, to be released later.

You need to decide how much heat storage to use. If you grow cool-weather plants, you need less heat storage. The amount of heat storage is also related to the size of the greenhouse. A small greenhouse loses more heat per unit of interior space than a larger one, so needs more storage. A greenhouse smaller than 150 square feet of floor space cannot hold much heat, and should be attached to a heated building such as your home.

Water is an effective heat-storage medium. Twice the volume, and four to five times the weight, of rock is required to store the same amount of heat as water. As a general rule for the Pacific Northwest, attached solar greenhouses should have 3 to 5 gallons of water heat storage per square foot of glazing. Freestanding greenhouses should have 5 to 7 gallons per square foot of glazing.

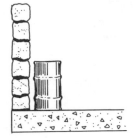

The rock wall, cement floor, and drums of water shown above are commonly used for heat storage. But soil in planting beds and the plants themselves store heat, as well.

Heat storage can gobble up space and be at cross-purposes with plant growth. Plants can shade light from heat-storage containers, and the containers can cut down on available light to plants, because they must be painted a dark color to absorb heat, while plants benefit from the light reflected off white surfaces. Keep in mind that soil beds that have been watered are about 50 percent as efficient as water in collecting heat and that plants are the most efficient solar collectors we know! You need to try out your greenhouse, and subtract as many heat-storage containers as possible while maintaining the temperature range you need.

An alternative to lots of heat storage is to use some type of night insulation on the glazing. The major heat loss from a greenhouse occurs at night through the glazing. Two-thirds of this heat loss can be reduced by using night insulation such as insulated curtains or shutters. This can free up more growing space in your greenhouse.

Living space. If part of the greenhouse is to become a green, sunny, living room, be realistic about the space needs for tables and chairs. Leave room to move around easily. If you have a nice view out the glazing, situate chairs so it can be enjoyed. The materials you use for flooring, insulating curtains, paints, and sealers can be beautiful as well as functional.

Walkways. Plan where to have walks and growing areas. In an aisle plan, plant areas run along both sides of the greenhouse, with an aisle between them. A peninsula plan has a main aisle running the length of the greenhouse, with narrower aisles reaching out to plant beds. Pathways should be 18 to 24 inches wide.

Planting beds. If you want to grow plants with deep root systems, planting beds can be used. You can make ground-level beds or elevated, contained beds. Ground-level beds are easier to make and can be used for growing taller plants, but may be uncomfortable because you must bend over. Elevated contained beds are more convenient to use, but require more materials and time to make. They are ideal for wheelchair access.

Aisle plan

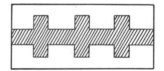

Peninsula plan

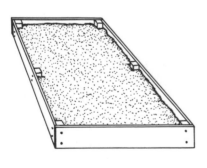

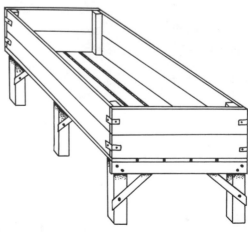

A ground-level bed can be enclosed by 2×6s for neatness. An elevated contained bed must be more sturdily built.

Ground-level beds should be prepared in the same manner described for outdoor raised beds, except even more soil supplements should be added because the beds will be used year round. Take care that the soil is kept free from contaminaton during construction of the greenhouse. You can keep the beds neat by enclosing the bed with 2-by-6 lumber. Drive 2-by-2 stakes deep into the ground along the perimeter of the bed and nail or bolt the 2-by-6s to them.

Elevated contained beds should be 18 to 24 inches deep. This requires sturdy construction because wet soil is very heavy. To provide drainage in a solid bottom, drill ½-inch holes at 6-inch intervals. If the botom is boards, leave gaps. Cover the bottom with nylon screen to hold the soil.

Benches. Benches (as the tables in a greenhouse are called) are used to support plants in containers. A simple way to make a bench is to lay boards on top of 55-gallon heat-storage drums. This platform will be more secure if you build a pallet of 1-by-4 lumber. Be sure to leave gaps between the slats for circulation.

There are dozens of ways to build freestanding benches. Any design should be sturdy, because just one 14-by-20-inch planting flat can weigh 25 pounds when filled with wet soil. A comfortable width for benches is 32 to 36 inches if they can be reached

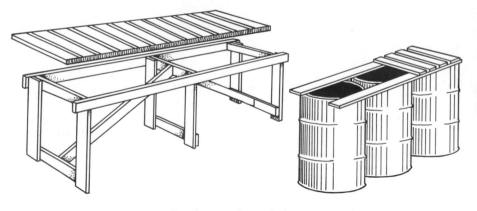

Benches can be made by simply laying boards on top of storage drums or by building any sturdy design from lumber.

from only one side and 42 to 48 inches if they can be reached from both sides. An example of a simple bench design uses 2-by-4 legs, braces, horizontal supports, and 1-by-2 lumber on top.

Work space. The inside of the greenhouse needs to include a work area where plants can be handled, pots washed, tools stored, and fertilizers mixed. Cupboards, a sink, good light, and room to move easily should be provided in this area.

Using the Vertical Space

Next, it is important to make diagrams of the vertical space. Heat storage and plants will be the major uses of this space, so be aware of the potential conflicts between them.

Shelves. Shelves permit you to use all the environments of your greenhouse. Plants that need heat and sun can fit on high shelves near the glazing, while shade-lovers will fit in nooks under benches or in dark corners.

Moveable shelves on metal tracks and brackets allow you to adapt to changing seasons and different heights of plants. If you don't plan to move shelves, metal brackets work well. If you want, you can use ¼" glass shelves to let more sunlight filter through. Any shelf you use will carry more weight without bending, if the supports are not right at the end of the shelf.

Experiment with structures to increase your usable vertical space. For instance, some people at the Cheyenne Community Greenhouse designed a shelf that fits over container beds and swings up to double as a trellis.

Trellises. Plants can be trained to grow on wires or wooden latticework to take advantage of vertical space. This will greatly increase the productivity of your greenhouse. To decrease shading, trellises can be oriented north–south or located along the north wall of the greenhouse.

Hanging plants. Plant hangers will expand the productive greenhouse space. The leaves of hanging plants also do a beautiful job of filtering glaring sunlight to a soothing level in your living space.

It is simplest to hang plants by their pots. The best ones we found were plastic with a snap-on

Hanging plants, shelves, and trellises help to make use of the vertical space.

saucer that catches water overflow. Some have hangers already attached; others you will have to suspend using wire or twine under the rim. Space at least three strands around the rim and connect them at a junction a foot or so above the pot.

If you want to add a decorative touch by putting pots in baskets, you should protect the baskets from water damage. Place a saucer under the pot inside the basket to catch overflow.

Finishing Materials That Work Well and Enhance Appearance

Flooring. Ground space that is not used for growing still needs to be finished in some way. The surface material should allow water to percolate into the subfloor, so concrete, which is impermeable, must be sloped and have drains. Flagstone or brick, dry-laid in several inches of masonry sand packed smoothly onto a base of sharp gravel, will make an elegant and functional surface for a mixed living/growing space. You can build slatted wooden paths over pea gravel for a comfortable walking surface, or simply have smooth gravel.

Paints and preservatives. Wood that is in contact with soil should be treated to prevent rot. Avoid wood preservatives that contain creosote or pentachlorophenol ("penta"), because these materials kill plants. Copper napthenate (sold under the trade names of Cuprinol and Cuprolignum) is safer, but one to two months should elapse to cure treated wood before planting. It is also expensive.

A preservative that is inexpensive and non-toxic is non-fibered asphalt emulsion (fibered asphalt contains asbestos fibers and should not be used). This material goes on with a brush, and plant beds can be used after it dries, usually in one or two days. It makes a good seal for concrete and brick, and has no odor. It can become tacky in hot weather, so it should not be used for walking surfaces or on places that you might brush against.

Humidity is high in greenhouses, and condensation occurs frequently. If fir, pine, or plywood are used, paint all exposed surfaces with an exterior-grade finish. Think of this step as interior design, and make the interior colorful and attractive, as well as functional. Cedar and redwood have natural pre-

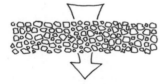

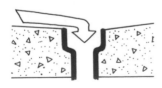

Loose flooring, like gravel or brick, allows water to filter through, while concrete floors must be sloped and have drains.

servatives and may be used unfinished, although white paint is desirable to improve light levels.

Insulating curtains and shutters. You should have one or the other to conserve heat at night. Insulating curtains work best on vertical glazing. On tilted glazing they are difficult to install, hard to use, and condensation inside the glazing wall will stain the fabric. This fact should be considered in choosing the glazing angle of the greenhouse. You need to look at the latest available products in internal and external shutters and weigh their pros and cons. At Amity's greenhouse we used large external styrofoam shutters that doubled as reflectors, but they took up a lot of ground space that could have been used for cold frames or cloches.

Designing for the Best Light Conditions

Each kind of plant differs in its light requirements. The intensity of the light (commonly measured in foot-candles or watts) must be correct for a particular plant. Most vegetables need at least 1,000 foot-candles, while 2,500 foot-candles is optimum for rapid, heavy growth. Most foliage plants need only 200 to 500 foot-candles. Flowering plants require 500 to 1,000 foot-candles of light. The daylength, or hours of duration, of the light is particularly important for flowering and fruiting plants. Most fruiting vegetables and flowering plants need 10 to 12 hours of light per day at their required level, while foliage plants can get by with less.

Horticultural textbooks, such as *Greenhouse Operation and Management*, by P.V. Nelson, cover light in great detail. What is most important is that you know your plants' needs and do not deprive them of light by overcrowding, by poor design, or by using the wrong part of the greenhouse.

Design and layout. You can affect the quantity of available light by design. Although the material you select for glazing affects the amount of light available for your plants, other design features may be even more important. The rafters supporting the glazing should be as narrow as possible, to reduce their shadows. The depth of the opaque walls to the east and west, and the opaque overhang of the roof, can make the difference between a dark cave and a light greenhouse.

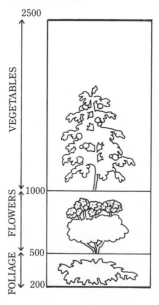

FOOT-CANDLES

2500

VEGETABLES

FLOWERS

FOLIAGE

1000

500

200

The layout has a great influence on light, as well. The location of heat storage, shelves, tall plants, hanging plants, and trellises is crucial. As the environment varies throughout the year with the changing sun angle, it is a challenge to use the space to its maximum potential.

Paint and reflectors. You can enhance light levels by painting the majority of the interior white. Heat-storage containers should remain dark to absorb heat.

Reflectors can also increase light. However, we found that in the cloudy Willamette Valley, reflectors were of minor value. We experimented on the Amity greenhouse, using large foil reflectors in front of the glazing. On a clear winter day, light was enhanced by as much as 22 percent. On a cloudy day reflectors did not help. Because clear days are infrequent during the winter, the expense and the space used by the reflectors is questionable. The amount of cloudy weather in your area should influence your decision to use reflectors.

Supplemental light. During cloudy winters, light levels are too low for active plant growth. Also, more light, and longer daylengths of light are required for fruiting and flowering of many desirable greenhouse plants. If you want to grow these plants, supplemental lights will be very helpful. You need to decide if the additional production justifies the cost.

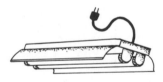

The familiar fluorescent lamp is particularly useful in propagation, while a high-intensity-discharge lamp stimulates flowering and fruiting of larger plants.

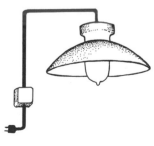

There are three types of lights: incandescent, fluorescent, and high intensity discharge (HID).

Incandescent bulbs, while low in cost, emit a red light which causes tall, soft growth of plants. They only convert 7 percent of the electrical energy into light, and most of the remainder is converted into heat. They are of limited value in growing.

Fluorescent lamps are over three times more efficient at converting electrical energy into light, and they burn up to 15 times longer than incandescent lamps. They must be kept within 2 to 3 inches of plants, so they are most useful for starting small seedlings or propagating cuttings. Some special types have been designed especially for plants (such trade names as Growlux, Agrolite, or Vitalite). These bulbs give off 40 percent less total light and

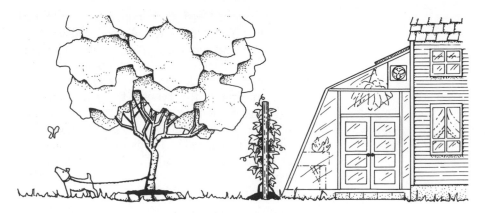

Deciduous trees and vines provide shade in the summer and allow full sun in the winter when it is needed.

are more expensive than standard fluorescent tubes. If you use one cool-white and one warm-white standard tube, you will achieve a balanced light spectrum and good growth at a lower price.

High-intensity-discharge (HID) lamps can be used for tall crops, since they can be placed 6 to 9 feet away from the plants. They can be used to stimulate flowering and fruiting. These powerful lamps are expensive, but require half as much wattage as fluorescent bulbs per lumen and last up to 50 percent longer.

Shade. In the winter you need more light, but in the summer you need shade. Depending on local weather, you may need shade as early as May 1.

Place shading on the outside of the glazing to intercept the light before it enters the greenhouse. If shades are inside, the greenhouse can still overheat because of the greenhouse effect.

Natural vegetation is an attractive way to provide shade. A deciduous tree in front of the greenhouse will shade from the summer sun, and when the winter sun is low, the bare branches and trunk will cast little shade. Avoid trees that come into leaf early (poplar, apple) or drop leaves late (beech, English oak, liquidambar). You may also trellis a deciduous annual vine outside. Grapes, morning glories, sweet peas, beans, hops, cucumbers, or rambling roses are some possibilities. Separate the trellis from the greenhouse by a foot or so, and be sure the trellis is strong enough to support the mature vines.

You can also provide shade by covering the glazing with a shade cloth, which can be bought at a gardening store. One type is a fiberglass screen that comes in different densities. A good density is 45 percent (the percentage of solar energy blocked). Alternatively, a lattice of wood, or a bamboo screen, can be used to block 40 to 50 percent of the sun.

An alternative to screens is temporary paint on the glazing. White latex paint diluted 1:15 with water provides a good shade. One product, called Vari-Shade, can be painted on the glazing and varies with light conditions. On rainy days it becomes transparent and on dry days it turns white to reflect sunlight and provide shade.

Any shading material or paint should be completely removed in September or October.

Designing for Good Air Quality

Vents. Solar greenhouses need to be well ventilated. Venting reduces heat, replenishes carbon dioxide, rids the greenhouse of excess moisture, and prevents conditions that could promote the buildup of mold and fungus.

The best locations for vents are near the peak of the roof and near the ground, unobstructed by shrubbery. Cool air is drawn in through the low vents while warm, moist air exits through the high vents. The rate of air circulation depends on the difference between inside and outside temperatures, the height difference between vents, and the size of the vent openings. As each increases, so does the ventilation rate. A 6-foot difference between high and low vents is desirable, and their size should be roughly 15 percent of the total floor area of the greenhouse. To maintain good air flow, the high vents should be about ⅓ larger than the lower ones.

Vents can be placed in doors, especially if the doors are at opposite ends of the greenhouse, and a fan-forced vent is used at the peak. All vents should be weatherstripped and caulked so they do not leak when they are closed.

Automatic vent openers can save you time and worry. Some are controlled by an electric thermostat, and others open by means of a piston that expands as temperatures warm the fluid inside. Vents fitted with vent openers can be set to open at a certain temperature. Remember that the temperature

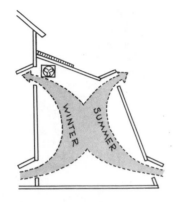

Cool air comes in through low vents, while warm air escapes through high vents. In the winter, this heat can be circulated into the house.

There are several types of automatic vent openers which are temperature sensitive.

near the roof vent will be warmer than the plants in the beds below it, so the vent-opening temperature should be selected for the best temperature at the plant level.

Fans. Venting is often all you need for adequate air circulation, but during the coldest months, constant venting loses too much heat. A fan located at the peak of the greenhouse and directed toward the plant level improves air quality when vents are closed.

A fan directed into a perforated plastic tube suspended along the peak of the greenhouse will improve the recirculation of warm air substantially. These tube systems are available through greenhouse suppliers.

Watering Systems

You should determine where water-supply pipes and drain systems will go, before building your greenhouse. It is often much easier to put water systems in at the beginning of construction than later. Install enough faucets so you can easily water all parts of the greenhouse.

Whatever systems you design, you should take care not to direct water onto surfaces that are not treated to resist water penetration. Another need is to have a floor that drains well. Puddles are unsanitary and hazardous. When these needs are taken care of, you may try out a variety of watering systems.

Hand-watering. We find hand-watering to be easy and effective, since we are in the greenhouse on a daily basis. We use a watering can or hose, with various nozzles that can deliver a flow ranging from a fine mist to a low-pressure, high-volume flow. A watering wand is needed for overhead plants and makes watering ground-level beds or wide benches easier.

Drip irrigation. These systems have strengths and weaknesses. They conserve water, but they also can clog, and thus require careful monitoring. Many systems are now on the market, and if you are interested, be sure to shop around. All of them are characterized by the use of small tubes, called emitters, that deliver water either to individual containers or to individual plants in a planting bed. All can

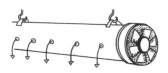

A fan attached to a plastic air duct can be suspended from the greenhouse peak for better air circulation.

Drip irrigation brings a trickle of water to each plant through a small tube.

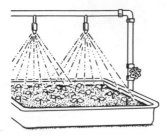

A misting unit is an efficient tool for keeping seedlings moist.

be connected to sensors and timers for complete automation.

Perforated hoses. Another type of watering system uses perforated hoses. They go under various trade names like Dew Hose, Ooze-Header, and Twin-Wall Hose. The hose is laid down the length of a plant bed and water oozes or drips out slowly to thoroughly water the soil at set intervals.

Mat watering. This is a good system if you have different sizes of pots. It uses a mat about ½ inch thick which is kept constantly moist. Pots are set on the mat and water is taken up by capillary action. A main advantage to this system is that pots of different sizes can be irrigated on the same bed. Several brands are available through garden suppliers. European gardeners simply use four to six layers of newspaper spread on a plastic sheet.

Misting. A pipe with fine nozzles can be set up over a row of plants to deliver a fine mist. Misting is excellent for propagating seedlings and cuttings and maintains the humidity required by young plants. It also helps to cool the greenhouse in the summer. Misting is not so useful for large plants which can suffer mold problems from constantly damp foliage and which require deep watering.

The Value of Professional Design Assistance

Many people enjoy doing their own designing and building. However, if you plan to attach a greenhouse to your home, you should consider whether you need skilled help. A poorly designed and constructed greenhouse can decrease the value of your home. There are now many solar greenhouse designers and contractors in the Northwest. You may save a lot of money and time in the long run by investing in their assistance.

Whether you go it alone or utilize assistance, you should be able to design a greenhouse that can be integrated fully into your daily life, if you consider and plan for the design issues we have reviewed.

Managing the Greenhouse for the Best Results

Management of a productive solar greenhouse and of a conventional greenhouse are similar in many ways. Plants need to be watered and fertilized, they sometimes need to be moved or repotted, and the greenhouse needs to be cleaned and repaired. There are some subtle differences in doing these tasks in the two types of greenhouse, which we'll discuss. The two differ most, though, with respect to temperature regulation and ventilation.

Temperature Regulation

A solar greenhouse relies on conservation and release of heat produced by the greenhouse effect. You need to control the loss of heat in the winter by closing vents and doors, using insulating covers at night, adding heat storage, and, if needed, installing a supplemental heat source. You may have to release heat at other times of the year by opening vents and installing shades to limit heat input. All management should be based on knowing inside temperatures by using simple devices and keeping records.

If you find it difficult or impossible to sustain the heat range you need for the plants you want to grow, you should first be sure all vents, doors, and

cracks are weatherstripped and sealed and the entire perimeter of the greenhouse is insulated. If you are certain it is completely weathersealed, you need to think about adding supplemental heat.

For an attached greenhouse, this may mean simply improving the movement of warmer air from the home to the greenhouse during cold, cloudy weather. This may require additional vents or fans. You may want to install a small, efficient wood stove, taking great care that plants are not near enough to be damaged by the intense radiant heat. In a freestanding greenhouse, you may decide to add a bed of fresh, comosting manure, and cover it with plastic to contain the odor. Electric heat may be expensive if used a great deal, but if it is only a small space heater used for 3 or 4 hours on a half dozen of the coldest, cloudiest days of the year, the expense can be considered well spent if it means carrying a good crop through. The fan used for air circulation should be used to circulate heat when your supplemental source is being used.

Heating the soil instead of the air is an efficient way to promote plant growth. Soil heat cables are available commercially. New designs are very efficient and easy to install. You may combine an existing heat source (wood stove or furnace) with a water coil system that runs through the soil. Each system varies in cost, efficiency, and ease of installation.

Ventilation

Ventilation provides air movement and air exchange which reduce humidity, bring in cooler air, and discourage mold. If plants are thriving in most of the greenhouse but a small pocket contains various plants suffering from either mold (indicating cool, still air) or wilt (indicating hot air), you should suspect circulation problems.

It was stressed in Chapter 6 that the greenhouse must be designed and built with good vent locations and the interior layout must provide good air circulation. Fans can be used to improve air movement, and you can add perforated plastic tubes designed especially for larger greenhouses for even more elaborate and effective control of air movement.

You will vent a solar greenhouse less than a conventional one in the winter because you will be con-

Max/min thermometer

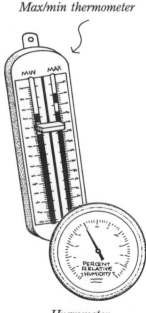

Hygrometer

serving the warm air more carefully. This will cause the humidity to be higher, so watering needs will be less, while fungus and mildew problems may be more likely. You will need excellent air circulation to keep plants healthy. You may not be able to put plants as close together as in a conventional greenhouse, and a fan may be needed to deal with high humidity.

Whatever equipment you decide to use, you should observe your greenhouse, document the temperatures in different zones, and experiment with cycles of ventilating and circulating air to find the best system.

Environmental Monitoring Tools

A few useful instruments will help you to observe the performance of your greenhouse. To measure air temperature you should use a maximum/minimum thermometer, which records the highest and lowest temperatures between each reading. It has to be shaded from direct sunlight and placed at the plant level. You may want three thermometers: one for bench level, another for the level where plants are hanging, and one on the outside of the greenhouse so you can see how the greenhouse and exterior temperatures differ. A good max/min thermometer will cost around $25, but you can buy a less accurate one for about $12 (all costs are based on 1989 prices).

Soil temperature is another measurement you should make. It is crucial for seed germination and affects plant growth, because the rate of nutrient uptake is dependent on soil temperature and soil moisture. Temperatures cooler than optimum will slow growth and encourage disease, while warmer temperatures may result in spindly growth. When you take soil temperature readings, the soil thermometer can be moved to different parts of the greenhouse, but wait at least five minutes between readings so the thermometer has a chance to equilibrate to its new surroundings. A soil thermometer will cost between $10 and $25.

Relative humidity, the percent of water vapor in the air, is important to plant growth and health.

Soil thermometer

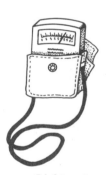

Light meter

Generally, the humidity should be between 40 percent and 75 percent. If it is too low, plants can wilt and show poor growth. Humidity above 80 percent encourages leaf mold and stem rot, and promotes the growth of foilage rather than fruit. The easiest way to measure humidity is with a dial hygrometer that can be mounted on a wall. A good hygrometer will cost around $20.

Because plants have different light requirements, you should match the light environment of the greenhouse with the needs of the plant. A light meter will enable you to quickly determine the different light levels in your greenhouse. If you are unprepared to spend $15–$20 and up for a light meter, you can use the light meter in a camera. Set the shutter speed at $\frac{1}{60}$ of a second and the ASA at 25 and point the camera at a sheet of white paper set in the area you are measuring. Get close enough to the paper that it is all you can see through the camera. Adjust the f-stop for the proper exposure. The f-stop will tell you how many foot-candles of light there are.

f-stop	2	2.8	4	5.6	8	11	16
Illumination (foot-candles)	100	200	370	750	1,500	2,800	5,000

Keeping Records

Each solar greenhouse has its own special environment, and you will have to discover the peculiarities of your own greenhouse. The best way to do this is through observation, experimentation, and record keeping. You will want to keep environmental and cultural records. Use a loose-leaf binder with section dividers to organize the different events you want to record.

To learn about your greenhouse, you should keep track of its various environments. This information will help you to select what to grow and where to grow it, and to plan your planting schedules. You can draw up a chart and photocopy enough for months of use. Here is an example of a chart to use for monitoring the environment.

Date and Time	Inside Temp °F Max/Min	Outside Temp °F Max/Min	Soil Temp °F Max/Min	Percent Humidity	Light	Outside Weather	Comment

The best way to make sense of all this environmental information is to draw up the monthly averages on a graph. Compare greenhouse and outside conditions on one graph. You will then be able to anticipate needs, such as when to ventilate longer, or when to put up insulating shutters, when the same weather patterns occur again. This will help you to regulate the greenhouse more smoothly. Some examples of ways to do this are presented here. These are summary data from readings taken at the Amity greenhouse.

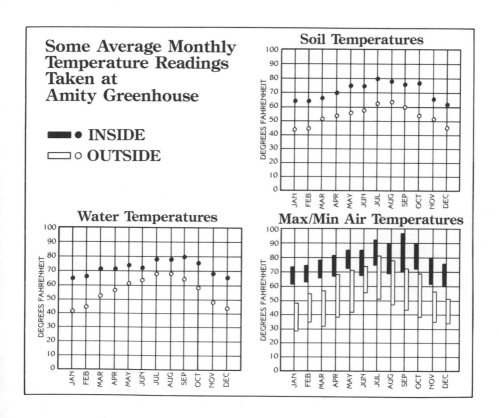

Planting Maps

For the Amity greenhouse we make planting maps and simple charts to learn better ways to grow plants. A planting map is just a bird's-eye view of a planting area. You sketch out what you want to plant and where, and plan for successions and rotations. Because a solar greenhouse makes use of vertical space, you will need a map for each level. For example, a greenhouse that has three levels (hanging or shelf level, bench level, ground level) would need three maps.

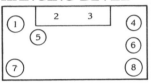

HANGING LEVEL

Location	Plant
1.	_____
2.	_____
etc.	_____

BENCH LEVEL

Location	Plant
1.	_____
2.	_____
etc.	_____

GROUND LEVEL

Location	Plant
1.	_____
2.	_____
etc.	_____

Plant Culture Records

With simple charts you can easily keep track of what has been planted and when, harvest dates, fertilizer application, and pest and disease problems. Leave lots of room for comments. Charts are useful because they make recording and finding information easy. You will be surprised how useful they can be later on. Here are a few examples of forms you can set up to simplify your record keeping.

VEGETABLES

Vegetable	Variety	Source	Start Date	Transplant Date	Greenhouse Location	Harvest Dates	Harvest Amount	Comment

HERBS AND ORNAMENTALS

Plant	Variety	Source	Propagation Date	Propagation Method	Greenhouse Location	Cultural Notes

FERTILIZER APPLICATIONS

Date	Type of Fertilizer	Plant Applied to	Amount	Greenhouse Location	Result	Comment

PESTS AND DISEASES

Date	Observed Pest or Disease	Plant	Damage	Control Measures	Result	Comment

Greenhouse Sanitation

The closed environment of a greenhouse is not only good for plant growth but is also ideal for some pests and diseases. Proper sanitation and regular observation are needed to control problems before they become epidemics. We have found the following practices to be most effective in ensuring healthy plant growth.

1. Keep the inside of your greenhouse and surrounding outside area clean. Cut down weeds that are nearby, because many insects and diseases live on these weeds. Remove dead leaves and fallen fruit from greenhouse beds to prevent mold and mildew from developing and to eliminate breeding grounds for other diseases and pests.

2. Provide your plants with a healthy environment. Provide a rich soil to encourage rapid growth. Don't overwater, since it will kill roots and weaken plants. Vent regularly; stagnant, moist air promotes disease. Screen greenhouse vents to reduce the chance of pest infestation.

3. Do not keep diseased plants in the greenhouse. If your prized tomato plant is covered with whiteflies and nothing you do helps, remove it from the greenhouse. Plants infested with a disease or pest may spread infection to other plants.

4. Constantly remove dead leaves and other debris. This decaying material makes an ideal breeding ground for pests and diseases.

5. Inspect new plants for insects and diseases. If possible, place them in quarantine in your home in a suitable environment for a week or two to make sure they are healthy. Alternatively, have a part of the greenhouse empty where you can hold them.

6. Don't overcrowd plants. When plants are overcrowded, air circulation is poor and plants are more prone to problems.

7. When reusing pots, disinfect them first. Soak used pots for a few minutes in a 10 percent bleach solution (1 part bleach to 9 parts water). It's a good idea to also disinfect your tools, especially if they have been around sick plants.

8. Water early in the day, avoid watering the leaves, and do not overwater.

9. Do not allow the end of the hose used for watering to touch plants or, more importantly, soil. Disease organisms, especially root rots and molds, can be picked up and transferred to other plants.

10. During the summer, when the greenhouse is in its lowest use period, go over the entire greenhouse to repair and clean it. Go through shelves and check all supplies and reorder for the upcoming season. Clean and sharpen tools, and paint anything needing paint. Check weather-stripping and seals for damage. Repair hoses, wash glazing, and remove all weeds. Test all the equipment to be sure it works properly and check the roof for damage. This annual maintenance period will revitalize your greenhouse and leave it fresh and ready for a new year of growing.

Greenhouse Watering

Watering needs vary according to greenhouse conditions, the size of containers used, the type of soil and soil depth, and the kind of plants you grow. Some general recommendations are:

1. Water when needed. Stick your finger or trowel into the soil to see if the soil is dry 6 to 7 inches below the surface. It is safer to let the soil dry out a bit between watering than to keep it wet all the time. Plant roots cannot get enough oxygen from soil that is constantly wet. The damaged roots cannot absorb nutrients or water and, as a consequence, the plants become stunted and wilt.

2. Water more when the weather is sunny and warm. You may find that you need to water

Summer is a good time for necessary cleaning and repair of the greenhouse and equipment.

once or twice every day during sunny periods, while during cool overcast months, watering may be needed only weekly.

3. Water thoroughly. As a general rule, apply ½ gallon of water to each square foot of bed space for every 8 inches of soil depth. Apply enough water to potted plants so it starts to run out of the bottom. This promotes deep root growth and helps prevent excessive buildup of fertilizer salts.

4. If your soil mix develops cracks, it has too much clay and your plants will suffer. Make a new soil mix and repot your plants, transplanting the root ball but leaving as much of the poor soil behind as possible.

5. Water in the morning. Plants are actively growing during the day and need the water to absorb nutrients. Watering in the morning also lets the leaves dry out before evening and reduces the chance of mold and mildew developing.

6. Water with gentle pressure. You don't want to wash the soil off the plant roots or to compact the soil.

Fertilizers and Pest and Disease Control

Chapters 13 and 14 will cover soil fertility, and pests and diseases. The practices of fertilizing and pest and disease control that will make you a successful open-air gardener also apply to greenhouse gardening. Your gardening success will also improve as you learn more about the special needs of each type of plant.

Special Soil Mixtures for the Greenhouse

Most soil in the Pacific Northwest has a high clay content. Under continual warmth, watering, and handling, field soil in your greenhouse will gradually come to resemble concrete. The solution is to radically change the character of the soil by amending it, or even to use a soilless mixture for certain purposes. The following are soil blends we found effective at the Amity greenhouse.

Seeding mixtures. One option is to buy a bagged sterile soil mix for starting seeds. Another option is to make your own soil mix. We prepare a "homemade" soil mixture by blending:

1 part topsoil
1 part coarse sand or perlite
1 part compost

This mixture is sifted through a 2-by-2-foot screen made of ¼" hardware cloth stapled to a frame of 1-by-4 lumber.

A fungus found in many soils destroys the stems of very young plants. This is called damping off. Commercial greenhouse operators kill the fungus by pasteurizing soil. This is generally done using steam mixed with air to 140°–160° F, which is forced through soil covered by plastic, for 30 minutes. The heat also kills weed seeds.

You can pasteurize small quantities of soil in the oven by baking a moist soil mixture in a shallow tray with the oven set on low. Cover the mixture to reduce the odor, stick a soil or meat thermometer into the center of the mix and bake at about 180° F for 30 minutes. We have used both pasteurized and unpasteurized soil and had equally good success. Your soil mix may be relatively free of pathogens, and it may be worthwhile to first try growing seedlings without soil pasteurization. If damping off becomes a problem, then you will have to pasteurize your soil or buy sterile mixes.

Another alternative is to use a "soilless" mix and thus avoid weeds and pathogens. A mixture of 1 part peat moss, 1 part vermiculite, and a sprinkling of steamed bone meal has been reported as a fine mixture for starting seeds.

Container soil mixes. We use the same soil mixture for containers from the size of our deep container beds to 2-inch pots for transplants. Herbs, ornamentals, and vegetables all thrive. We amend the deep beds with a generous dose of fertilizers before planting as noted below.

The basic soil mixture is:
1 part soil sifted through a ¼" sieve
1 part compost or worm castings sifted through
    a ¼" sieve
1 part sand or perlite
½–1 cup ground limestone per 5 gallons soil mix.

For cactus, use 2 parts sand or perlite in this mix. Orchids require special mixtures that you can buy at gardening stores.

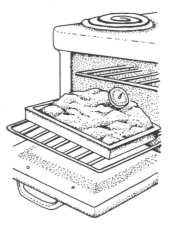

Soil can be baked in the home oven to kill fungus and weed seeds.

To provide a good level of fertility, we use the following amendments for every 50 square feet of raised container beds:

2 lb. cottonseed meal or bone meal

2 lb. bone meal

1 lb. wood ash

3 lb. powdered limestone or dolomite

Soil for ground-level beds. The ground-level beds in the greenhouse should have a lot of organic matter and sand or perlite incorporated to provide a productive base for your inside gardening. Peat moss, leaf mold, rotted hemlock bark, and well-rotted horse or cow manure are good sources of organic matter. As you dig and prepare the bed, spade in one spadeful each of sand and organic matter for each square foot of planting bed.

Replace the top 3 to 6 inches of a greenhouse planting bed with a fresh soil mix once or twice a year and repot plants regularly. Your plants will appreciate it and you should not have as many pests or nutrient problems.

Plant Propagation

One of the best uses of a solar greenhouse is to propagate plants to be used later in the open-air garden, beautify the house, to give to friends, or even to sell. There are a variety of shady and sunny zones in a solar greenhouse, each one perfect for a different stage of plant propagation. This brief survey will simply emphasize the value of your greenhouse in multiplying plants. Several wonderfully illustrated texts give the reader lots of information on technique (see *Plant Propagation*, P.M. Browse, and *Plant Propagation in Pictures*, M. Free).

Sowing Seed

Most vegetables and many common garden flowers are grown from seed each year. You will want to have space with good warmth and light for this use, as the soil temperature needs to be in the 60° to 70° F range for many of these plants. The water supply to these areas should be set up so you can keep the seed flats moist at all times. Easy access is crucial, as the flats will need to be moved for transplanting.

Temperature: Rapid germination of most flower and vegetable seeds takes place at soil temperatures of 65° to 85° F. At temperatures of 50° F or less, germination is slow, if it occurs at all. At low temperatures, fungi attack and kill young seedlings. Dryness or excessive heat will kill a seedling, stunt its growth, or cause it to bolt (finish its growing cycle prematurely). Regulate temperatures in your solar greenhouse by adding or subtracting heat storage, using a fan, and venting carefully. The cost of a thermostatically controlled vent may be a useful investment, if you cannot be at the greenhouse enough to regulate temperature manually.

Watering: Seedlings need a soft, moist soil surface that they can break through. Water the soil surface by using a watering can with a fine watering

Seedlings must be watered with a fine mist.

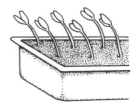

Spindly plants bending toward the light need some help from an artificial light.

head, or use a mist nozzle on a hose. After seed-lings emerge, use this system, or stand the container in a shallow bath of water and let the water seep upward through the container to the surface. Remove the container from the bath after the soil is thoroughly wet.

Keep the mixture moist, and when plants begin to emerge, place them in sunlight. Be very careful to check the moisture in the soil, and water when it begins to dry out. On warm days this may be two or three times per day when seedlings are very young. (Drip irrigation can simplify this watering and help guarantee steady plant growth. See Chapter 6.)

Light: When seeds germinate, they require good light for growth. If needed, move them to a sunny bench or shelf. The plants wil bend toward the light, so turn the containers daily to keep the plants growing upright. If the sky is heavily over-cast and your plants are spindly and/or pale, you may want to use artificial light to grow the seedling to transplant size (see Chapter 6).

Transplanting

Seedlings are generally started very close to-gether and do not need nutrient-rich soil. They are transplanted to give them nutrients and growing space for both leaf and root development. We prefer to transplant into individual pots because it is easier to plant these into the garden. Transplant when plants develop their first true leaves. Do not confuse the seed leaves, which are first to emerge, with the true leaves. The true leaves will have veins, while the seed leaves won't.

Before transplanting, water the seedlings to moisten the root balls so they will remain intact when removed. You may need to thin the seedlings so each one has at least one square inch of soil. Snip off excess plants with small scissors. With a knife, cut through the soil and roots, and then lift out the seedlings under the soil. Be gentle and careful. If necessary, support the upper part by a leaf. Never pinch the stem, because the plant will die or become stunted if the stem is damaged.

Place the seedling in a hole in the soil of the new container. Firm the soil around each plant and

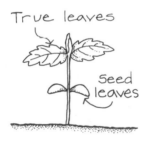

True leaves

Seed leaves

water gently. Do not expose the new transplants to direct light for a few days. It is best to water in the morning and, if possible, water with a weak manure tea or fish-emulsion solution.

When seedlings are ready to be planted to the open garden or cloche, harden them off if needed, and transplant carefully.

Starting Plants from Cuttings and Divisions

Seeds are not the only way you can increase your supply of plants. Another method, called vegetative propagation, enables you to grow a new plant from part of a "parent" plant. Pieces of stem, root, or leaf can be used to grow a plant identical to the parent it was taken from. Plants can also be propagated from runners, bulbs, and root divisions. (The books on propagation by Browse and Free are, once again, excellent references.) A solar greenhouse is a perfect place for this type of plant multiplication.

All these sources of new plants rely on the same conditions: a good rooting medium, warmth, moisture, and light. The best conditions for propagating are a soil temperature around 65°–75° F and very high humidity. Direct unfiltered sunlight is harmful; a partly shaded or screened area is best. The upper shady part of the greenhouse may provide these conditions.

You can also build a simple propagating chamber, which is just a small cloche inside your greenhouse. This will help to maintain high humidity.

Making a hole in the soil for the roots of the new transplant.

If soil temperatures stay below 60° F, you can improve soil heat by using a heating cable. Place the heating cable in a 3-inch to 4-inch layer of sand and set the planting flats on top of the sand. Heating cables are best used under a propagating chamber, because the heat is contained. By carefully following the instructions for making cuttings and divisions, you can have hundreds of starts. Care of plant starts is virtually the same no matter which method of propagation is used. The plants should be watered with a fine spray or mist once or twice a day and transplanted when the roots are ¼ inch to ½ inch long. Check by gently lifting one cutting out of the rooting medium. Grow the young plants in the greenhouse locations most suited to their needs for sun, shade, heat, or coolness.

A homemade propagating chamber can be made from 2×2s and plastic sheeting, and filled with a commercial heating coil.

Vegetable Gardening

You can grow almost any vegetable you want in a solar greenhouse if you are aware of the needs of the plant and understand the environment of your greenhouse. At any one time a solar greenhouse has spots that are warm or cool, sunny or shady, the locations of which change seasonally. You need to regulate the conditions in the greenhouse and plant those vegetables that are best suited to each zone. The following diagrams show where those zones would be located in one solar greenhouse.

Vegetable Layout

In planning the layout of your greenhouse vegetable garden you must not only think of light and heat, but also consider the height of each plant and the growing space it requires. Most seed catalogs give the mature size of each kind.

If you trellis plants that sprawl, you will free up bed areas. Crops that can be trellised include beans, cucumbers, melons, peas, squash, and tomatoes. Consider using the space shaded by tall plants for growing smaller semi–shade-tolerant plants such as lettuce or carrots. Be sure to leave enough room for each plant to reach its mature size. Experience will

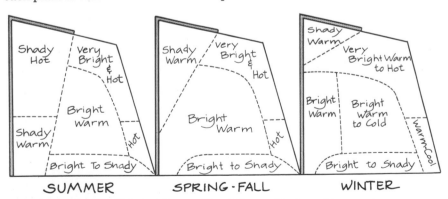

Seasonal Variations Inside a Solar Greenhouse
Adapted from S. Smith, *The Bountiful Solar Greenhouse.*

be your best teacher in learning about the space requirements in your greenhouse.

When planning your layout and planting schedule, leave some open planting space, so you can plant in a series of staggered plantings. You can then have fresh vegetables over a long period.

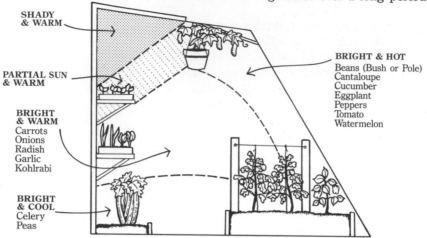

SHADY & WARM

PARTIAL SUN & WARM

BRIGHT & WARM
Carrots
Onions
Radish
Garlic
Kohlrabi

BRIGHT & COOL
Celery
Peas

BRIGHT & HOT
Beans (Bush or Pole)
Cantaloupe
Cucumber
Eggplant
Peppers
Tomato
Watermelon

Should You Use a Cloche or a Greenhouse?

Any vegetable that can be grown in a cloche or cold frame may also be grown in a solar greenhouse. What we found, though, in surveying the Northwest, was that a cloche can produce a better crop of many cool or cool-to-warm vegetables than the greenhouse, which may tend to be too warm unless it is closely managed. For example, it is much less expensive to grow broccoli under a cloche, and if the crop from the cloche tastes and produces better, why use a greenhouse?

Size can be a factor also. The large size of vegetables such as cauliflower limits the number of plants in a greenhouse, while a cloche can easily cover many large plants.

Think twice about using a greenhouse for growing crops that take a long time to mature, such as cabbage and most root crops except radishes. Seed catalogs list the time to maturity, but this is for ideal temperatures and light conditions. It will take longer than this for crops grown under less than ideal conditions. Many slow-growing vegetables do very well under a cloche or cold frame. At the Amity gardens we have shifted more and more of our year-round vegetable production out of the greenhouse and into cloches and cold frames without much loss of production.

As a greenhouse gardener, you need to be aware of these facts. You can produce warm-temperature crops in a winter greenhouse, and you can also have fresh aromatic herbs and cut flowers. Neither cold frame nor cloche has enough heat storage to permit these uses. You can have a convenient fingertip source of small root crops like beets or carrots and not use up all the greenhouse space, since they produce when small. View the greenhouse as the source of special treats that can't be grown in a cloche or cold frame or that can produce a more tasty crop, and you will put your greenhouse to good use!

Size is a consideration in choosing vegetables for the greenhouse.

Vegetable Planting and Harvesting Schedule

There are now a number of seed catalogs that carry vegetable varieties especially suited to greenhouse conditions. (Some of these companies are listed in Appendix A.) New varieties are available every season. During our Northwest survey, we found that when the same vegetable variety was grown in different greenhouses, one greenhouse grower would

Vegetable Growing Seasons in a Solar Greenhouse
Adapted from S. Smith, *The Bountiful Solar Greenhouse.*

This timetable is based on a cloudy winter schedule, that is, a winter monthly average of less than 45% possible sunshine as listed by your closest National Weather Service.

P=month to plant			M=growing to maturity				H=harvest time				

CROP	Jan.	Feb.	Mar.	Apr.	May	June	July	Aug.	Sep.	Oct.	Nov.	Dec.
						MONTHS						
Beans—Bush		P	PM	PMH	PMH	PMH	PMH	PMH	PMH	MH	H	
Beans—Pole				P	PM	PMH	PMH	MH	MH	H	H	
Cantaloupe				P	PM	PM	MH	MH	MH	MH	H	
Carrots	PMH	PMH	PMH	PMH	PMH	PMH	PMH	PMH	PMH	PMH	PMH	PMH
Celery	PMH	MH	MH	MH	H			P	PM	PMH	PMH	MH
Cucumber			P	PM	PM	PMH	PMH	MH	MH	MH	H	
Eggplant				P	PM	PMH	MH	MH	H			
Garlic	MH	MH	PMH	PMH	PMH	PMH	PMH	PMH	PMH	PMH	MH	MH
Kohlrabi	MH	MH	PMH	PMH	MH	H		P	PMH	PMH	PMH	MH
Lettuce	PMH	PMH	PMH	PMH	MH	H		P	PMH	PMH	PMH	MH

	1	2	3	4	5	6	7	8	9	10	11	12
Onions, Green	PMH	PMH	PMH	PMH	PMH	PMH	PMH	PMH	PMH	PMH	PMH	PMH
Peas	MH	PMH	PMH	MH	H		P	PM	PMH	PMH	PMH	MH
Pepper					P	PM	PMH	PMH	MH	MH	H	H
Radish	PMH	PMH	PMH	PMH	PMH	H		P	PMH	PMH	PMH	PMH
Tomato			P	PM	PMH	PMH	PMH	PMH	MH	MH	H	
Watermelon					P	PM	PM	MH	MH	MH	H	

Pinching the suckers off a tomato plant (above), and a sturdy support system (below).

report success while another would report failure. Growing records were not clear enough to pinpoint causes. Each solar greenhouse has unique characteristics which may affect variety success.

There is a wide latitude possible for planting and harvesting in a solar greenhouse, as the following chart suggests. You can provide the vegetables you choose with the correct environment.

Vegetables Requiring Special Greenhouse Management Techniques

Crops that did well in our greenhouse and that need special growing guidelines are tomatoes, European cucumbers, and melons. All three need supplemental light in the winter to give them the 12 hours of light per day necessary for bearing fruit.

Tomatoes. Many varieties of tomatoes are available, but the greenhouse varieties (Vendor, Tropic, and others) are particularly well suited to greenhouse conditions. They are resistant to many diseases commonly found in greenhouses, have a good yield (about 10 pounds per plant), and can be trained vertically to use space economically.

Tomatoes need daytime air temperatures between 70° and 80° F and night temperatures above 60° F. Soil temperatures should remain above 65° F. Each plant should be given at least 4 square feet of room and should be kept pruned at 6 to 7 feet tall.

An easy way to support greenhouse tomatoes is to run a strong galvanized or plastic-coated wire 2 feet above the row of plants. The wire must be connected to very strong hardware, screwed or bolted to the walls or stable posts. Tie a sturdy support string to the wire for each plant. As the tomato grows, wind it around the string, or use plastic clips, available at garden stores, to hold it. This support system can also be used for cucumbers and climbing beans and peas.

Greenhouse tomatoes need pruning to ensure a high yield and to prevent them from taking over the greenhouse. Pruning involves pinching off secondary stems, or "suckers," that grow from the notch between a leaf branch and the main stem. Be careful not to prune the tip of the main stem. If it is pruned, the tomato stops growing and you'll have to train a sucker stem up the string if you want any more new tomatoes.

During harvest, remove the leaves below the lowest tomato to increase air circulation to the plants. Tomatoes grown in the greenhouse will need to be pollinated by hand.

European Cucumbers. The best type of cucumber to grow in a greenhouse is the European cucumber. It is very productive, resistant to many common greenhouse diseases, and, unlike garden varieties, does not require pollination. Seeds for the European cuke are expensive, but each plant can bear 40 or more fruit, with each fruit reaching up to 16 inches long.

A. *Removing the flowers from a young cucumber promotes plant growth.*

European cucumbers will begin producing fruit when the plant is young. This will stunt the plant and yield will be low. For best yields, pinch off young fruit until the plant is 4 to 5 feet tall. One mature plant requires 7 to 10 square feet of space and should be trained to about 7 feet and pruned as shown.

Cucumbers like a high relative humidity and lots of water. They also need more nitrogen and require warmer temperatures than tomatoes. The air temperature should not drop below 65° F at night and should be between 75° and 85° F during the day. The soil temperature should remain above 65° F.

Melons. We have had a lot of fun growing cantaloupe and watermelons in the Amity greenhouse. They reach maturity by midsummer and are a real conversation piece when visitors drop by.

B. *Pruning the growing points when the cucumber plant reaches optimum height.*

Melons need to be trellised or they will sprawl all over the greenhouse. You can buy a ready-made trellis or make one out of 1-by-1s or wooden lath. If you want to reduce their shading effect, the trellis should run north–south in the greenhouse. The plants should be spaced about 3 feet apart.

When the melons flower, you will have to pollinate them. As the fruits develop, provide support by enclosing them in a mesh (nylon stockings or cheese-

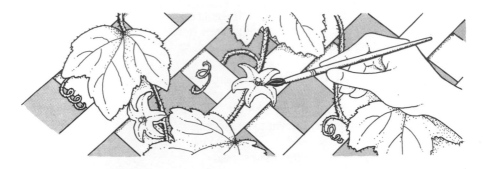

Pollinating a melon plant
with a paintbrush. Some
plants, such as tomatoes or
peppers, only need a tap of
the finger on the blossoms.

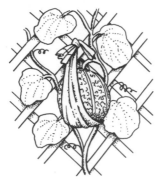

*Melons grown on a trellis
need some extra support.*

cloth work well) that is tied securely to the trellis.

Look for varieties resistant to wilt and mildew, and choose the smaller watermelon varieties. We have had good luck with Harper Hybrid cantaloupe and Sugar Baby watermelons.

Pollination

Pollination, the transfer of pollen from the male flower to the female flower, is required to make plants set fruit. Outdoors it is done by wind and insects, but inside a greenhouse the plants need your help.

Some plants have both male and female parts in the same blossom. These plants include tomato, eggplant, okra, and pepper. Vibrating the plant is all that is needed to move pollen the short distance from the male to the female part. Tap each of the flowers with a finger or stick. Conditions are usually best for pollination between 11:00 a.m. and 2 p.m. when the humidity is low enough for the pollen to shake loose.

Other types of plants have separate male and female blossoms. Look for a tiny fruit behind the female blossom. The pollen must be transported from the male blossom to the female blossom. Twirl a small paintbrush inside the male blossom to pick up pollen. Then stroke the stalk inside the female flower with the pollen-laden brush. This should be done to cucumbers (other than European greenhouse varieties) and melons. If pollination did not occur, the blossom and fruit will wither and die.

Growing Herbs

Herbs are perfect for growing in containers in a greenhouse. Most herbs thrive in sun, and they not only add colorful foliage, delicate blossoms, and sublte fragrances, but also have culinary, nutritional, and medicinal uses. High-quality herbs can be grown in a greenhouse, while the cool, wet climate of the maritime Northwest prevents many herbs grown out-of-doors from developing strong oils and fragrance. Many can be grown out of season in the greenhouse, while others will flourish in the greenhouse during the heat of summer.

Generally, herbs require bright sunlight, good air circulation, and a soil that can dry between thorough waterings. Most do best with low nutrient levels in the soil. Some can only be propagated by cuttings, but many others are available as seeds. Each herb has different germination needs.

Many herbs will become lanky or tend to sprawl unless they are pruned frequently. Pinching the tips maintains a full bushy shape.

There are hundreds of herbs to choose from. Those that we chose to include are herbs that we have seen thriving in Northwest greenhouses. The list offers types for all the zones of the greenhouse, and a variety of texture, shape, use, and fragrance. Those that are winter-hardy can be grown year round outside, but you can also enjoy them in comfort in your warm greenhouse, when outside in the garden the icy winds blow.

Basil

An annual that grows to a height of about 1 foot. Start from seed and transplant 2 or 3 plants to 5-inch pots or grow 6 inches apart in beds. Basil does best in full sun with ample water. It has a sweet scent like tomato plants in the hot sun. Fresh leaves are popular for flavoring salads, sauces, vegetables, and soups and are great in tomato dishes. Leaves can be prepared in "pesto," a delicious sauce, and frozen

Basil

Burnet

Chamomile

Chervil

Chives

for quick use. If allowed to flower, it will go to seed and die, so pinch the tips back to prevent flowering and to keep it bushy.

Burnet

A perennial that will reach a height of 12 to 18 inches. Propagate from seed or by dividing the roots. Transplant 2 or 3 plants into 6- to 8-inch pots or grow 12 inches apart in beds. Burnet grows best in full sun and in a soil that is allowed to dry between waterings. Use young leaves in salads and sauces to give a cucumber flavor. Dried leaves are good in vinegar and make a fragrant tea.

Chamomile (German)

An annual that grows to a height of about 1 foot. Chamomile can be propagated from seeds (which are slow to germinate), cuttings, or by division of the plants. Transplant 2 plants per 10-inch pot, or grow 10 inches apart in a bed. It likes to be in full sun and well-drained soil that is allowed to dry between waterings. The flower heads make a relaxing tea with a scent of apple.

Chervil

This annual grows 1 to 2 feet in height. Start from seed in the pots they will be growing in, as they do not transplant well. Plant 1 plant to a 4-inch pot or 4 plants in an 8-inch pot; or grow 4 inches apart in beds. Chervil like partial shade and moist soil. The leaves are ready to use 6 weeks after planting. The deep green leaves are used like parsley and also make a mild tea.

Chives

A perennial of the onion family that grows to a height of 1 foot and has wonderful pompoms of lavender flowers. It is easy to grow from seed or by dividing clumps from mature plants and repotting into 4- to 6-inch pots or 6 inches apart in beds. Chives prefer lots of sun and plenty of water. The tender green leaves are used fresh to give a mild onion flavor to soups, salads, omelets, and other dishes. Will overwinter. Leaves can be diced and frozen in small packets. It produces best when the leaves are cut continuously.

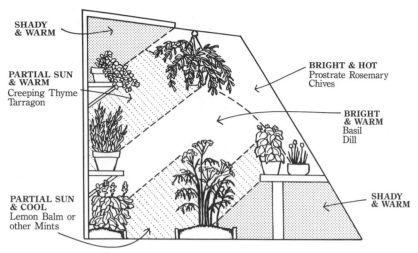

Locating Herbs to Best Suit Their Light and Heat Needs

These conditions would be found in the greenhouse during the spring or fall. When herbs are in pots they may easily be moved as the greenhouse environment changes with the seasons.

Dill

Lavender

Dill

An annual that can grow to 4 feet. A good variety for the greenhouse, Bouquet, is shorter and more erect than others. Dill does not transplant well, so seed directly into 6- to 8-inch pots or space 3 inches apart in beds. It likes lots of sun, but the soil should not be allowed to dry out, because the plant will flower before the leaves are fully grown. The leaves are used to flavor sauces, salads, and egg, cheese, and fish dishes. The ripe flower heads and dried seeds are used in pickling.

Lavender

Use the perennial dwarf and semi-dwarf varieties that reach a height of 12 to 18 inches. Two good varieties are Munstead Dwarf and Hidcote Purple. Lavender can be started by seed, cuttings, or division. Transplant 1 to 2 plants into 6- to 8-inch pots or grow 8 inches apart in beds. It needs full sun and gravelly soil that drains well. Lavender will add a delicate fragrance to your greenhouse. The dried flowers are used in sachets for linens and clothing.

Mint

Oregano

Parsley

Rosemary

Mint

There are many members of the mint family, ranging from Corsican Mint, a dwarf ½ inch high, up to lemon balm, a hardy perennial which can reach a height of 3 feet. Most types of mint can be started by seed but are easier to propagate from cuttings or pieces of root. Grow tall varieties in 8- to 10-inch pots and keep trimmed back to prevent them from becoming leggy. If grown in beds mint will spread rapidly. It does well in partial shade and likes lots of water. The various types include peppermint, spearmint, lemon balm, and horehound. There are also ornamental varieties with gold-edged or white-edged leaves. The strongly scented leaves are used in many Greek recipes, to spice vegetables and meat dishes, in cold drinks, to flavor liquors, and to make tea. Finely chopped fresh leaves can be used to make mint sauce and jelly.

Oregano

This perennial grows to a height of about 1 foot. Start from seeds or cuttings and transplant 4 to 5 seedlings in 8- to 10-inch pots or space 10 inches apart in beds. It is very hardy and does best in full sun and a moist soil. Keep it well trimmed to prevent it from sprawling. This is the familiar flavoring for Italian-style dishes. Use the leaves fresh or dried.

Parsley

Best grown as an annual, it will reach a height of 8 to 10 inches. Score and soak the seeds in warm water for a day before planting. Plant 2 to 4 plants in 8-inch pots or 8 inches apart in beds. Parsley can be grown in partial shade, and the soil should be allowed to dry between waterings. It can be used fresh or dried to enhance the flavor of any dish. Parsley is rich in iron and vitamin C.

Rosemary

A hardy perennial that grows slowly to a height of 2 or 3 feet. There are also prostrate forms that creep or trail. It is difficult to grow from seed, but easy to propagate with cuttings. Plant 2 or 3 plants to 6-inch pots or 12 inches apart in beds. Rosemary is pretty when cascading over a hanging basket or window box, with fragrant spikes of pale blue flowers. The leaves have a spicy aroma and provide a wonderful flavoring in soups, sauces, salads and meats.

Sage

A hardy perennial that grows to a height of 2 feet or more. It is easy to propagate from seeds and cuttings. Transplant 2 or 3 plants to 6-inch pots or 12 inches apart in beds. Keep sage in sun for continuous purple blooms and let soil dry between waterings. The unusual leaves make it a picturesque potted plant. There are lovely variegated types. The leaves can be used as a flavoring in dressings, sauces, and stuffings. Tea from the leaves is good for colds.

Sage

Savory, Summer

An annual that grows to about 18 inches high. Start from seeds and transplant 2 or 3 seedlings to a 6-inch pot or 10 inches apart in beds. Grow in full sun and let soil dry between waterings. The peppery leaves are used to add flavor to soups, salads, and sauces.

Savory, Winter

A perennial that grows to about 2 feet in height and has a better shape and appearance for ornamental growing than summer savory. It is covered with small pale lavender blossoms in the summer. It is best propagated by cuttings, since seeds are slow to germinate. Transplant to 6- to 8-inch pots or 12 inches apart in beds. Like summer savory, it likes full sun and a light, dry soil. The leaves can be used like summer savory, but have a stronger flavor.

Winter Savory

Sorrel

A hardy perennial that grows to a height of 2 to 3 feet. Propagate from seed or by dividing roots. Plant in 6-inch pots or space 12 inches apart in beds. It can be grown in full sun or partial shade and likes to be kept moist. The heart-shaped succulent leaves can be used fresh in salads and soups or cooked and eaten like spinach. It is very high in Vitamin C. French varieties have much larger and tastier foliage.

Sorrel

Sweet Marjoram

Sweet Marjoram

A perennial that grows to a height of 8 to 12 inches. It is easy to start from seed or cuttings. Transplant to 6-inch pots or 10 inches apart in beds. Give it lots of sun and let the soil dry between waterings. The delicate aromatic leaf is used in soups, salads, dressings, stuffings, sauces, and vinegar.

Tarragon

Tarragon

A perennial that grows 1 to 2 feet in height. True French tarragon cannot be grown from seed and is propagated from cuttings and root division. Transplant 2 to 3 plants to 8-inch pots or grow 12 inches apart in beds. Grow in partial shade and let the soil dry between waterings. Use the leaves fresh to flavor salads, poultry, fish, sauces, and vinegar. It has a flavor similar to anise.

Thyme

Thyme

A low-growing perennial that reaches a height of about 1 foot. Dwarf varieties and creeping varieties provide a range of choices of form and texture. Transplant 3 or 4 plants to 6-inch pots or grow as a border plant in beds. Keep in full to partial sun and let the soil dry out between waterings. Keep pruned to encourage bushy growth. The highly aromatic flavor of the leaves makes thyme one of the most popular herbs. Use fresh or dried leaves to flavor soups, chowder, salads, fish, and meats.

Growing Ornamental Plants

The beauty of ornamental flowering and foliage plants will attract you into your greenhouse often. You can bring your loveliest plants of each season into other parts of the home and spread the pleasure of the greenhouse around. By choosing the right kind of plant, you can have flowers in bloom year round and, unlike a lot of vegetables, many foliage plants tolerate shade and are robust dring the low light levels of winter.

Growing Ornamentals in Pots

There are many advantages to growing individual plants in their own containers. The plants can be watered and fertilized as each requires and can easily be moved to the best light and heat zone as the solar greenhouse environment changes. Plants in containers need some special attention to do best.

Potted plants do not have much soil to draw nutrients from. To keep the plants healthy, you need to fertilize them regularly. Some types of plants require special commercial fertilizers, which will include instructions for use.

If you want your plant to grow larger, you should repot it when it grows slowly despite ample light,

A plant must be repotted periodically if it is to grow larger.

Anemone

Crocus

Lily

Tulip

Forcing Spring Bulbs

One of the most satisfying activities in a greenhouse is forcing spring bulbs, which is simply beguiling them into blooming weeks or months earlier than they would bloom naturally outside. Bulbs can be potted anytime from September to December and will bloom from February to April.

Here are some simple steps for forcing some popular bulbs.

1. Most bulbs should be stored in the refrigerator for several weeks before planting.
2. Plant bulbs in pots in clusters of 3, 4, or 5, in good potting soil.
3. Water the soil well and store the pot in a shady and protected location outside.
4. Cover the pots with a thick layer of leaves or straw, or place in a cold frame to protect from freezing.
5. When shoots appear 8 to 12 weeks later, put the pots in a shady place in the greenhouse, start to water, and gradually move the plants into full light. Keep well watered.
6. After the plants bloom, keep them in sun or partial shade and allow the leaves to flourish, wilt, and then die away naturally. The leaves rebuild the food reserves.
7. Most bulbs cannot be forced 2 years in a row. Plant forced bulbs in the open garden after one season in the greenhouse.

Hyacinth

Amaryllis

Daffodil

Iris

water, and fertilizer. Repot, also, when roots grow from the drain holes or if roots are thickly matted and coiled around one another.

If you want to keep a plant at a certain size, you can cleanly trim off some of the old roots, repot the plant in the old pot with new soil, and pinch back the top growth.

Growing Guidelines for Ornamentals

We talked with Pacific Northwest greenhouse gardeners and searched many books to come up with the following list of ornamental plants and their growing guidelines. These plants are proven to do well in Northwest solar greenhouses. We have included types with different environmental needs so you can grow plants in all the zones of the greenhouse. We also chose them to provide you with year-round color and a variety of sizes, shapes, and foliage textures for your gardening pleasure. It is a seed list, a way to orient you to putting all of your greenhouse to use all year round. An excellent reference to take you further is *Rodale's Encyclopedia of Indoor Gardening*, edited by A.M. Halpin.

The plants are grouped so that you will find all those that will do well in a particular zone in one cluster. The zones are: Bright and Hot, Bright and Warm, Bright and Cool, Partial Sun and Warm, Partial Sun and Cool, Shady and Warm, and Shady and Cool.

A cool zone has day temperatures to 70° F and night temperatures 40°–55° F. A warm zone has day temperatures to 75° F and night temperatures 65°–55° F. A hot zone has day temperatures above 75° F and night temperatures above 65° F. Many plants can tolerate wider ranges (unless noted otherwise). We have included temperatures for optimum growth in case you are interested in using the greenhouse exclusively for growing one or a few types in large numbers.

Plant sizes are listed as follows: small plants are 0 to 6 inches; medium plants are 6 to 18 inches; large plants are over 18 inches.

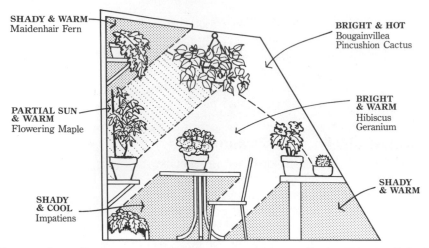

SHADY & WARM
Maidenhair Fern

BRIGHT & HOT
Bougainvillea
Pincushion Cactus

PARTIAL SUN
& WARM
Flowering Maple

BRIGHT
& WARM
Hibiscus
Geranium

SHADY
& COOL
Impatiens

SHADY
& WARM

Locating Ornamental Plants to Best Suit Their Light and Heat Needs

These conditions would be found in the greenhouse during spring or fall. When plants are in pots, they may easily be moved as the greenhouse environment changes with the seasons. Ornamental plants make your living space more beautiful if carefully selected.

Bright and Hot

Black-eyed Susan Vine (*Thunbergia*)

VARIETIES: *T. alata*
TEMPERATURES: 70°–80° F (day); 60°–65° F (night).
CULTURE: Keep soil moist; use well-drained soil; remove dead flowers to prolong blooming; hanging basket, vine; blooms summer to winter.
SIZE: Medium to large.
FORM: Trailing.

Bougainvillea, Paper Flower (*Bougainvillea*)

VARIETIES: *B. glabra, B. spectabilis*
TEMPERATURES: 65°–80° F (day); 60°–65° F (night).
CULTURE: Let soil dry between waterings; pinch off dead blooms to prolong flowering; vigorous climber; prune back after blooming.
SIZE: Medium to large.
FORM: Upright or climbing.

Pincushion Cactus *(Coryphantha)*

VARIETIES: *C. bumamma, C. clava, C. elephantidens*
TEMPERATURES: 80°–90° F (day); can go below freezing at night.
CULTURE: Let soil dry between waterings; can take very cold temperatures; blooms summer to fall; good for pots.
SIZE: Small to medium.
FORM: Rounded.

Stonecrop *(Sedum)*

VARIETIES: *S. adolphi, S. hirsutum, S. morganianum, S. rubrotinctum*
TEMPERATURES: 65°–80° F (day); 50°–65° F (night).
SIZE: Small to medium.
FORM: Rounded or trailing.

Bright and Warm

Geranium *(Pelargonium)*

VARIETIES: 280 varieties, many colors and scented leaves.
TEMPERATURES: 65°–75° F (day); 60°–65° F (night).
CULTURE: Let soil dry between waterings; needs 4 hours direct daylight daily for full flowering; will flower spring to winter with enough light; prefers to be potbound.
SIZE: Medium.
FORM: Rounded to upright.

Hibiscus, Rose Mallow *(Hibiscus)*

VARIETIES: *H. rosa-sinensis, H. schizopetalus*
TEMPERATURES: 65°–70° F (day); 50°–55° F (night).
CULTURE: Keep soil moist; prune to maintain shape; can bloom almost all year with full winter sun; fertilize monthly during growing season; partial sun in summer.
SIZE: Medium to large.
FORM: Upright.

Jasmine *(Jasminum)*

VARIETIES: *J. mesnyi, J. officinale, J. polyanthum*
TEMPERATURES: 60°–70° F (day); 50°–60° F (night).
CULTURE: Keep soil moist; pinch back frequently to maintain shape; fragrant white flowers, spring to summer; vine or pot with support; tolerates full sunlight.
SIZE: Medium to large.
FORM: Upright or climbing.

Lantana *(Lantana)*

VARIETIES: *L. camara, L. montevidensis*
TEMPERATURES: 65°–75° F (day); 55°–60° F (night).
CULTURE: Let soil dry between waterings; likes to be potbound; pinch back to shape plant; too much fertilizer reduces bloom; blooms fall to winter; cut back in summer; hanging basket.
SIZE: Medium.
FORM: Upright and rounded.

Pinwheel Cactus *(Aeonium)*

VARIETIES: *A. arboreum, A. decorum, A. haworthii, A. nobile*
TEMPERATURES: 45°–70° F (day); can go below freezing at night.
CULTURE: Let soil dry between waterings; does well potbound; blooms spring to summer; plant dies after blooming; needs good ventilation.
SIZE: Medium.
FORM: Loosely rounded.

Bright and Cool

Chrysanthemum *(Chrysanthemum)*

VARIETIES: *C. carinatum, C. coronarium, C. morifolium*
TEMPERATURES: 60°–65° F (day); 40°–50° F (night).
CULTURE: Keep soil moist; needs 12–14 hours darkness for 8–10 weeks to flower; good for cut flowers; cut stems back after blooming.
SIZE: Small to large.
FORM: Rounded to upright.

Citrus Fruit *(Citrus)*

VARIETIES: *C. aurantifolia* (lime), *C. aurantium* (sour orange), *C. limon* (lemon), *C. sinensis* (sweet orange)
TEMPERATURES: 65°–75° F (day); 45°–55° F (night).
CULTURE: Keep soil moist; flowers must be hand pollinated; dwarf root stock available; plant in pots at least 18 inches across; use slightly acid soil.
SIZE: Medium to large.
FORM: Upright.

Field Marigold *(Calendula)*

VARIETIES: *C. officinalis*
TEMPERATURES: 55°–65° F (day); 40°–50° F (night).
CULTURE: Keep soil moist; good drainage important; does well in cool greenhouse; for summer blooms, sow in spring; for spring blooms, sow in fall; remove dead flowers to prolong bloom.
SIZE: Medium to large.
FORM: Loosely rounded.

Sweet Pea *(Lathyrus)*

VARIETIES: *L. odoratus*
TEMPERATURES: 65°–75° F (day); 50°–60° F (night).
CULTURE: Keep soil moist; many hybrids to choose from for year-round bloom; provide trellis, string, or wire for support.
SIZE: Large.
FORM: Climbing.

Partial Sun and Warm

African Violet *(Saintpaulia)*

VARIETIES: *S. confusa, S. grotei, S. ionantha, S. shumensis*
TEMPERATURES: 65°–80° F (day); 60°–65° F (night).
CULTURE: Let soil dry between waterings; blooms best when potbound; blooms year round; full sun, winter.
SIZE: Small.
FORM: Rounded.

Bellflower, Star of Bethlehem *(Campanula)*

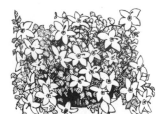

VARIETIES: *C. elatines, C. fragilis, C. isophylla, C. poscharskyana*
TEMPERATURES: 50°–70° F (day); 50°–65° F (night).
CULTURE: Let soil dry between waterings; likes rich organic soil; blooms spring–fall; trim stems back after flowering; hanging baskets or trellis; full sun, winter.
SIZE: Medium.
FORM: Trailing or climbing.

Cattleya Orchid *(Cattleya)*

VARIETIES: *C. bowringiana, C. gaskelliana, C. intermedia, C. labiata, C. mossiae, C. percivaliana*
TEMPERATURES: 70°–80° F (day); 55° F (night).
CULTURE: Let soil dry between waterings; after flowers open, reduce water and fertilizer; blooms spring to winter; hanging basket or pot; full sun, winter.
SIZE: Medium.
FORM: Loosely rounded to upright.

Coffee Plant *(Coffea)*

VARIETIES: *C. arabica*
TEMPERATURES: 70°–75° F (day); 65°–70° F (night).
CULTURE: Keep soil moist but not soggy; does not like to be potbound; pinch stems to keep shape and encourage bloom; tree 4–6 feet tall.
SIZE: Medium to large.
FORM: Upright.

Flowering Maple *(Abutilon)*

VARIETIES: *A. hybridum, A. megapotamicum, A. pictum*
TEMPERATURES: 65°–75° F (day); 55°–65° F (night).
CULTURE: Keep soil moist, but not soggy; will flower at temperatures down to 55° F; blooms spring to fall; cut back after flowering to retain shape; hanging basket or train along pole.
SIZE: Large.
FORM: Upright and trailing.

Grape Ivy *(Cissus)*

VARIETIES: *C. rhombifolia*
TEMPERATURES: 68°–75° F (day); 60°–65° F (night).
CULTURE: Keep soil moist; dark green foliage; hanging basket; prune in spring to keep shape; not fussy about soil or fertilizer.
SIZE: Medium to large.
FORM: Trailing.

Jade Plant *(Crassula)*

VARIETIES: *C. argentea*
TEMPERATURES: 68°–75° F (day); 50°–55° F (night).
CULTURE: Keep soil moist but not soggy; good container plant; blooms winter to spring; full sun, winter.
SIZE: Small to large.
FORM: Rounded to upright.

Partial Sun and Cool

African Daisy *(Gerbera)*

VARIETIES: *G. jamesonii*
TEMPERATURES: 65°–70° F (day); 55°–60° F (night).
CULTURE: Let soil dry between waterings; blooms spring to winter; good for cut flowers; partial warm areas good also.
SIZE: Medium.
FORM: Loosely rounded.

Camellia *(Camellia)*

VARIETIES: *C. japonica*
TEMPERATURES: 60°–70° F (day); 40°–45° F (night).
CULTURE: Keep soil moist; high humidity and good ventilation; does well in cool greenhouse; remove dead flowers to prolong bloom; good for cut flowers; shrub or tree; blooms spring to winter.
SIZE: Medium to large.
FORM: Upright.

Primrose *(Primula)*

VARIETIES: *P. malacoides, P. obconica, P. sinensis, P. veris*
TEMPERATURES: 55°–60° F (day); 40°–50° F (night).
CULTURE: Keep soil moist; does not like to be potbound; blooms winter to spring; remove dead flowers to prolong blooming.
SIZE: Medium.
FORM: Rounded.

Shady and Warm

Fibrous Begonia *(Begonia)*

VARIETIES: *B. metallica, B. Rex-cultorum, B. scharffii, B. semperflorens,* and many other varieties
TEMPERATURES: 65°–75° F (day); 50°–60° F (night).
CULTURE: Keep soil moist; use soil rich in organics; best growth and flowering when roots are potbound; fertilize weekly during growing season.
SIZE: All sizes.
FORM: Rounded to trailing.

Split-leaf Philodendron *(Monstera)*

VARIETIES: *M. deliciosa*
TEMPERATURES: 70°–80° F (day); 60°–70° F (night).
CULTURE: Let soil dry between waterings; prefers to be potbound; needs large pot with support; can grow 15 to 20 feet tall.
SIZE: Large.
FORM: Upright or climbing.

Maidenhair Fern *(Adiantum)*

VARIETIES: *A. raddianum*
TEMPERATURES: 75°–85° F (day); 60°–65° F (night).
CULTURE: Keep soil moist but not soggy; does best in pots just large enough to hold root ball; hanging basket or pot.
SIZE: Medium.
FORM: Trailing.

Shady and Cool

Fuchsia *(Fuchsia)*

VARIETIES: *F. fulgens, F. hybrida*
TEMPERATURES: 60°–70° F (day); 40°–60° F (night).
CULTURE: Keep soil moist; likes to be potbound; cut back after bloom; blooms summer to fall; hanging baskets.
SIZE: Medium.
FORM: Upright or trailing.

Impatiens *(Impatiens)*

VARIETIES: *I. platypetala, I. repens, I. walleriana*
TEMPERATURES: 60°–70° F (day); 50°–55° F (night).
CULTURE: Let soil dry between waterings; seed needs light to germinate; pinch back to promote flowering; can flower year round; beautiful in hanging baskets; fertilize when in active growth.
SIZE: Medium.
FORM: Rounded.

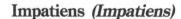

Hydroponics

Solar greenhouses use a heat-storage material to reduce the need for supplemental heating and cooling. Water is most frequently used because it's cheap, readily available, and stores more heat in less space than any other commonly available heat-storage material. But this volume still uses a lot of space in a greenhouse.

Amity has explored ways to use the water heat storage of solar greenhouses for food production as well. The first approach we tried was using the heat-storage water for raising edible fish. A handbook we published in 1979, *Fish Farming in Your Solar Greenhouse* (W. Head and J. Splane), describes our experiences. In 1980, we expanded the use of the greenhouse aquaculture water to include hydroponic gardening. Hydroponics is a method of growing crops without soil. The nutrients are supplied in a liquid form, circulated in a trough. Plants are supported so their roots are in the solution.

Most hydroponic systems rely heavily on synthetic fertilizers and relatively high energy and equipment costs. Nancy Volk of the Rodale Research Center found in a study that ready-made home hydroponic units did not produce vegetables at a price that was economically practical for the average home owner.

We investigated combining fish farming with hydroponic vegetable growing. In this system, fish supply the fertilizer for the plants in the form of uneaten food and nitrogen-rich waste by-products, and the plants help to keep the water clean by absorbing nutrients from the fish water. Ideally, additional fertilizers are not needed and equipment costs may be minimized.

We have had both success and failure, trying to make the concept work. Our simple hydroponic system used water from the 1700-gallon heat-storage tank in which we raised fish. The system had two trickling filters to recondition the water for the fish.

In hydroponic gardening, plants are supported with their roots in a trough of nutrient-rich water.

It was easy to connect PVC pipes to the filters to be used as hydroponic growing troughs. The pipes were suspended over the aquaculture tank and drained back into the tank. We cut out a 1½-inch-wide slot on top of each pipe, screened the ends, and filled the troughs with vermiculite to support the plants.

To our dismay, the vermiculite washed out when the water flowed into the pipes. We then tried pea gravel. Water flowed freely through the gravel and we transplanted 6-week-old tomato starts into the troughs. The tomatoes grew well and began to produce ripe fruit.

As the plants reached maturity, however, things went awry. Leaves wilted and died, stems turned brown, and roots rotted. The tomato roots had

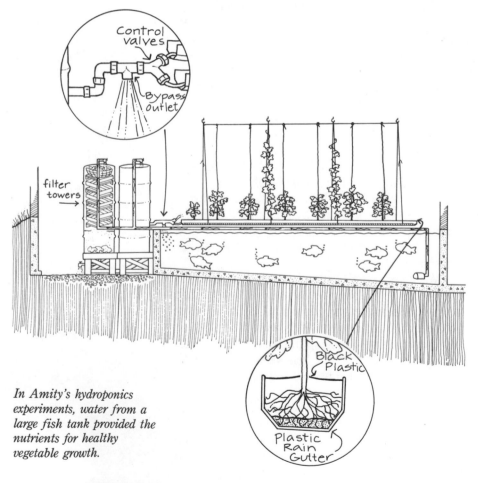

In Amity's hydroponics experiments, water from a large fish tank provided the nutrients for healthy vegetable growth.

grown so tightly around the pea gravel that they acted like a dam and blocked the water flow, causing the roots to suffocate. Undaunted, we replaced the pea gravel with ¾-inch volcanic rock, hoping a larger-diameter rock would correct the clogging. Our tomato yield doubled to about 5 pounds per plant, but after the plants matured, the roots again rotted.

We decided to try a different crop. We chose European cucumbers as our next crop. We got very good yields of about 11 pounds per plant, but once again root rot developed after the plants matured.

After this we redesigned the entire hydroponic system, incorporating a method called the Nutrient Film Technique (NFT). NFT can grow crops on much lower nutrient levels than are required in other hydroponic systems. This is particularly important for hydroponic designs, such as Amity's, that use only the relatively low nutrient levels of an aquaculture system. A shallow stream of nutrient water is circulated through a dense mat of plant roots. The upper roots in the mate are exposed to moist air. This provides both abundant nutrients and oxygen to the roots.

To switch to the NFT system, we made these design changes:

• We switched from a round PVC drain pipe to a plastic rain-gutter pipe with a flat bottom to spread out water more evenly.

• We installed plastic garden-hose valves to control the flow of the fish water so it left the hydroponics trough in a thin but continuous stream. Excess water from the filters was shunted into the fish tank through a downturned T-shaped PVC pipe fitting installed before the hose valve.

• The rock rooting medium was removed, which lowered both the cost and weight of the system and made the troughs more manageable and easier to clean.

• The tops of the troughs were covered with 4-mil black plastic to keep the roots moist and prevent the growth of algae.

We started tomato seeds in peat pots and vermiculite and in 4 weeks transplanted the plants and pots into the hydroponics troughs through slits made in the plastic. The peat pots provided support for the young plants and allowed the roots to grow into a common root mass. Each of the 3 hydroponics troughs held 8 tomato plants. The aquaculture tank was stocked with 60 small channel catfish (*Ictalurus punctatus*) and 120 African perch (*Tilapia mossambica*). The total initial stocking weight of fish was about 4 pounds.

Channel Catfish

African Perch

The fish were fed twice daily with a commercial fish pellet (Purina trout chow). The plants were irrigated entirely with the aquaculture water.

During a 7½-month testing period, 90 pounds of edible fish were harvested and each of the 24 tomato plants had an average yield of 9 pounds of tomatoes. Tomato plants of the same variety that were raised in the greenhouse soil yielded about 7 pounds of fruit per plant.

We were pleased with the performance of this design. It required less labor than crops growing in the soil beds, and we never had to worry about watering the plants. Water flowed freely along the pipes throughout the testing period and the roots were healthy, with abundant fine root hairs at final harvest.

A variety of people are interested in linking greenhouse components into more complex ecosystems. The New Alchemy Institute, located in Massachusetts, the Rodale Research Center, Recovery Systems, Inc., of New Mexico, and university research teams are some of those who are integrating fish culture and hydroponics to diversify greenhouse crops and increase productivity.

The New Alchemy Institute's experiments in raising vegetables using fish water have been a success deserving of mention. Crops that were raised included celery, tomatoes, lettuce, cucumber, and sweet basil. They got particularly good yields from tomatoes and European cucumbers. In one trial, 5 tomato plants from the hydroponic system yielded an average of 15 pounds of fruit per plant, and 5 European cucumber plants yielded an impressive 63 pounds of fruit per plant! New Alchemy's best hydroponic trial has produced about 2.3 pounds of vegetables per pound of fish food, plus the edible fish.

In both Amity's and New Alchemy's work the fish water provided the nutrients required for plant growth. Tissue analysis showed, however, that small additions of supplemental nutrients, particularly potassium, may be required to provide a full complement of essential plant nutrients.

Those of you who are adventurous enough to consider using your heat storage to raise fish should also consider growing vegetable or flower crops with the fish water. There is still a lot of work needed in order to refine the aquaculture-hydroponic connection. Current research may well encourage you to explore these possibilities.

Plant Health and Soil

Plant health is largely a reflection of the fit between the environment and a plant's genetic needs. Managing the amount of light, heat, cold, and moisture within a covered garden is an important element of plant health. Your management of the soil is also crucial. Since this is a fundamental garden skill, it will be summarized, just to remind you of the important facts. If you need more thorough information, check through the references in the appendix.

Plant Nutrition and Plant Health

Plants have the miraculous ability to photosynthesize—that is, to use the sun's energy to manufacture living matter. In order to do this, they need carbon dioxide, water, and 13 elements that must be drawn from the soil. Soil fertility is the term used to describe the soil's ability to provide these key elements.

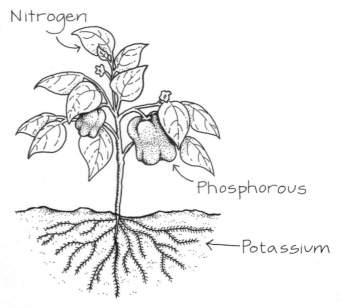

These elements are viewed as plant nutrients. Nitrogen (N), phosphorus (P), and potassium (K) are known as major plant nutrients because they are needed in large quantities by plants. The other nutrients needed are just as important for plant growth, but they are required in much smaller amounts.

1. Nitrogen: Nitrogen encourages rapid growth and healthy green leaves. Without enough nitrogen, plants are stunted and leaves turn yellow and drop off. With too much, the growth is soft and leaves develop at the expense of flowers and fruit. Nitrogen is rapidly leached from soil and needs to be replenished frequently. Manure, blood meal, and a variety of synthetic nitrate and ammonia compounds supply nitrogen.

2. Phosphorus: Phosphorus is especially important for early growth because it stimulates root formation. It is also a key nutrient in flower and fruit development. Plants with too little phosphorus are stunted and lose lower leaves. Bone meal, rock phosphate, or superphosphate supply phosphorus.

3. Potassium: Potassium, or potash, is required for sturdy growth, well-colored, healthy fruit, and especially for healthy root crops. It increases cold-hardiness and builds disease resistance. Lower leaves of a plant deficient in potassium will yellow along their edges, then exhibit brown spots, and finally fall off. Wood ash, green sand, and kelp supply potassium. Use wood ash in small amounts, for it has harmful salts.

4. Trace Elements: These elements are just as important as N, P, and K, but aren't required in such large amounts. One way to make sure calcium, magnesium, molybdenum, and others are present in adequate amounts is to add complex organic matter to the soil, such as compost from kitchen and garden waste. When you return the organic residue from living organisms, you are simply closing the circle of life. Feed the soil and the soil will feed you.

Tomato blossom end rot results from calcium deficiency.

Soil Testing

Soil needs to be well balanced with the proper nutrients for plant health. Soil used year round will become depleted regularly, but periodic soil tests can identify problems early. You can pay to have your soil tested or you can do it yourself. Kits that test for nitrogen, phosphorus, potassium, and pH cost around $40. These kits are relatively easy to use and have tables that tell you the correct amounts of fertilizers to add. You will need to adjust levels based on the plants and the season.

Other indicators of nutrient imbalance are pest problems and leaf condition. For example, aphids can be a sign of excess nitrogen, and the leaves of plants with too much nitrogen willbe dark green, and flower and fruit production will be curtailed. Spider mites can be a sign of calcium deficiency. Young leaf margins curl back and yellow, and in tomatoes the end of the fruit will rot. Entire texts are available with such diagnostic descriptions. The general gardening section of Appendix D lists some good books for diagnosing nutrient problems.

pH

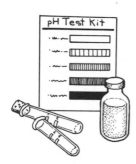

The acidity of the soil is measured in a unit known as pH. Both the chemical and biological release of soil nutrients are greatly affected by soil pH. Some plants, such as potatoes and many native ornamentals, like an acid soil, while most other vegetables, fruit trees, roses, and others prefer an almost neutral soil. Soil pH is measured on a scale from 0 to 14, with 7 considered neutral. A pH above 7 is alkaline, or sweet, and a pH below 7 is acid, or sour. You can measure the pH using a simple kit. If the pH is too low for the crops you are growing, you can add the recommended amounts of agricultural limestone or dolomite to neutralize it. If the pH is too high, adding sulpur will lower it.

Soil Building

Even the richest soil will become depleted of nutrients if it is used again and again to raise plants. Vegetables and many ornamentals are particularly greedy users of nutrients.

There are several ways to improve soil. Fertilizing adds a known quantity of a given nutrient, generally one of the major nutrients. Composting and green manuring add small quantities of nutrients while improving the texture, water-holding capacity, and drainage of soil. Since green manuring is largely of value to under-cover gardeners using a cloche, it is discussed in Chapter 5. Composting and fertilizing are of value for any type of gardening under cover.

Composting

Composting enables you to use kitchen and garden wastes and other available organic matter to renew your garden soil. Many writers have made composting appear so complicated that only a PhD in soil science could do it successfully! However, it is easy to do and is of immeasurable benefit to your garden. Here are some easy steps to get you started.

1. Select a space large enough for two piles side by side, each measuring at least 3' square. The piles need to be a cubic yard in size (3' by 3' by 3') in order to heat up. You may enclose them in any number of ingenious ways. If they are not enclosed, they will need more area to reach the required depth of 3 feet, so allow more room.

2. Vary the materials that you put in the pile. Two-thirds of the pile should be materials such as dry grass and weeds, leaves, straw, or sawdust, which are all high in carbon. One-third should be high in nitrogen, such as fresh green leaves (grass clippings, weeds), manures, and any kitchen waste except bones. If you are short on nitrogen materials, sprinkle in any high nitrogen source you would use for fertilizer. Add 2 cups of powdered limestone or dolomite to neutralize acids and to supply earthworms with calcium, which they require.

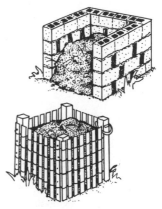

Compost can be made in almost any container that allows ventilation.

3. Mix the materials and chop big things up for faster composting. Some books have intricate instructions about layering a compost pile, but by thorough mixing you achieve the same purpose.

4. Water the pile if it is dry, so it is moist but not soggy, and cover it with plastic to retain heat and keep out excess rain.

5. As the pile grows, turn it, to hasten decomposition. For fast composting (6 to 8 weeks), the pile should be turned every week. You'll know it's working if the center of the pile is hot and steaming. For longer composting (3 to 6 months), turn after 4 weeks and 8 weeks. You will want to start a second pile as soon as you've gotten the first one going. Your finished compost will be dark and crumbly and have a pleasant earthy fragrance. You may need to add

worms dug from the garden if they haven't found the pile. Their activities help to finish compost.

Add the compost to your soil and you will be making a good base for sustaining your garden. The heavy demands of continuous gardening, though, require additional fertility. This is when fertilizers come into play.

Turning the compost pile speeds up the process and gives you a chance to check its progress.

Fertilizers

Fertilizers include powdered minerals, synthetic chemicals, organic remains of plants, including seaweed, and animal manures and by-products. Organic fertilizers differ from synthetic fertilizers in several ways. Most synthetic fertilizers are quick-acting because they have high levels of minerals and are water soluble. Some can be absorbed directly by the plant roots. However, these fertilizers are so concentrated that they may harm plants and they are also flushed out of the soil rapidly. Organic fertilizers have lower concentrations, and the minerals generally are held in reserve by soil bacteria before plants can use them. Organic fertilizers are slower-acting, but they are available to the plants over a longer period.

With the exception of blood meal, fertilizers do not work well in cool (50° to 60° F) soil. The bacteria that release nutrients just aren't very active at cold temperatures, and plants aren't active in nutrient uptake. Putting a cloche or cold frame over the soil will raise the temperature and increase bacterial activity and plant growth.

Most fertilizers are used to replace at least the major nutrients. Commercially available fertilizers (both organic and synthetic) have three numbers on the labels. These numbers indicate the percentages, by weight, of nitrogen (N), phosphorus (P), and potassium (K), in the order N:P:K. For example, 5:10:10 means the fertilizer is 5 percent nitrogen, 10 percent phosphorus, and 10 percent potassium, by weight. Sometimes a fourth number, indicating sulphur content, is also on the label. Manures vary in the percentage of nutrients. Many tables are available in books and extension bulletins that give estimates of the contents of manures and organic fertilizers.

Commercial fertilizers list the major elements by percentage, in this order: nitrogen, phosphorus, potassium.

Applying Fertilizers

If you apply fertilizers at the right times, you can increase your plant production tremendously. Many gardeners routinely mix fertilizers in soil before planting, as advised in gardening references. This is good practice for summer gardens, but crops that are planted late in the fall for overwintering should not be fertilized heavily until spring. Fertilizing in the fall can, in fact, weaken plants and threaten their survival through the winter.

Instead of mixing fertilizers throughout the soil bed before planting, we find it more economical to give a balanced fertilizer to each plant when it is transplanted and periodically throughout the growth cycle. These amendments can be applied either as a dry mix beside the plant (side-dressing), in solution in the irrigation water (manure tea), or in solution sprayed directly on the leaves (foliar fertilizing). These methods are particularly valuable for nutrients that are leached out rapidly. If synthetic fertilizers are applied, use them in very low concentrations and place them farther from the plant to prevent burning the roots.

The following are recommendations for fertilizing vegetables. Flowering plants also benefit from fertilizers.

Alliums: Benefit from nitrogen every 6 to 8 weeks.

Brassicas: Provide nitrogen 6 weeks after transplanting and again when heads begin to form.

Cucurbits: Provide nitrogen when vines begin to spread.

Greens: Provide nitrogen 3 to 4 weeks after transplanting and again just before maturity.

Legumes: Benefit from light additions of a balanced fertilizer.

Roots: Add phosphorus at transplanting. Root crops do not need nitrogen during growth cycle.

Solanaceae: Provide compost and bone meal 3 to 4 weeks after transplanting and after first fruit appears.

"Manure tea" is good for a quick boost to a particular plant.

Dealing with Pests and Diseases

Cloches, cold frames, and greenhouses create ideal environments not only for plant growth but also for pests and diseases. Rather than battling problems, you should practice prevention. You can go a long way toward this by developing good management habits. Follow the greenhouse sanitation recommendations described in Chapter 7 and these additional management tips:

1. Choose disease-resistant varieties. There are many vegetable varieties that are resistant to local diseases. Check the seed catalogs. New resistant varieties are available almost every season.

2. Use healthy transplants. If your transplants are weak, spindly, or stressed they will be more susceptible to pests and disease. If your plants start out healthy, they have a better chance of staying healthy.

3. Avoid planting at peak insect infestation times. By using protective coverings, you can miss many of the peak insect cycles (aphids, root maggot, cabbage moth, etc.). We have less insect damage on our late-fall and early-spring plantings because we miss the time when the insects are naturally at their peak numbers. Contact your local county agricultural extension agent to find out about peak insect times for your area.

4. Rotate your crops. By not planting the same crop in the same place every season, you can prevent buildup of pests and diseases in the soil and surrounding area.

Some vegetable varieties are practically immune to pests and diseases.

5. To kill soil-borne diseases and pest insects and their eggs in the soil, solarize outdoor garden plots (see Chapter 3). Leave the earth of greenhouse beds bare, and close the vents for a few weeks in August or when the weather is expected to be hot.

6. Spend time with your plants. They will tell you a lot about the particular conditions in your covered garden.

Controlling Pests

If insect problems do occur, there are several ways to handle them, including garden planning, home remedies, traps, biological controls, and commercial chemical pesticides.

Garden Planning

You can escape major problems by choosing crops that are relatively pest-free. If you grow highly susceptible plants, you must be prepared for a seasonal battle with insect pests. The following list rates vegetables for susceptibility to attack (from *Integrated Pest Management for the Home and Garden*, R. Metcalf, *et al.*).

Practically immune: beets, chard, Chinese cabbage, lettuce, radishes, peas, most herbs.

Few and minor problems: mustard, spinach, sweet potatoes.

One serious pest: asparagus, corn (early), onions, tomatoes.

A devastating enemy: beans, broccoli, cauliflower, cucumbers, eggplants, squash.

Several serious pests: cabbage, corn (late), melons, potatoes.

Home Remedies

Home remedies can be as varied as the gardener's imagination. They include such things as water and soap sprays, repellent concoctions, hand-picking, voodoo, threats, and a host of others.

One of the best remedies we have used for under-cover gardening has been the soap spray. Soap sprays are most effective on soft-bodied insects such as aphids, whiteflies, and spider mites. In some soaps there are fatty acids that will kill insects. Gardeners have reported good results using 2 tablespoons of Ivory liquid, Castile soap, or Basic-H in a gallon of water, or dissolving 1 ounce of Ivory flakes or Fels Naptha in a gallon of water. Put the solution in a spray bottle and spray the affected plant. Since soap sprays have no residual effect, at least 2 sprays a few days apart are required for control. You can harm plants with too strong a soap solution, so take care. There is now a commercial soap available, sold under the trade name of Safer's Insecticidal Soap, that we have found to be very effective.

Repellents such as garlic or cayenne pepper solutions can also be used for controlling most sucking and chewing insects. They create a distasteful environment, so the insect goes away. However, we have found that the soap sprays work just as well or better, and they are a lot easier to prepare.

Sometimes hand-picking is the most effective way of controlling insect pests. We have found this to be true for the garden slug. After trying everything from beer traps to slug bait, we found that our best control measure was to go out in the evening with a flashlight and remove as many slugs as we could find. This must be done nightly in the peak slug seasons of spring and fall.

Traps

Traps can be effective in keeping many pest populations below harmful levels. They work by luring the pests away from their normal habitat.

A common recommendation for the control of whitefly is to paint a board yellow, cover it with something sticky like vaseline or light grease, and hang it in an area where the flies are. The flies are attracted to the yellow color and will stick to the board. Yellow sticky fly paper works too. We have had only moderate success with this method. There are always more whiteflies on the plants than on the boards. The boards also do not affect the larval stage, which can be just as devastating to plants. We have had more success in controlling whiteflies using soap sprays.

whitefly Trap

Small boards can be placed on the soil surface to trap shelter-seeking insects such as slugs, weevils, sow bugs, and pill bugs. Each morning, check under the boards and remove the pests that have congregated there.

Earwigs can be captured by laying pieces of corrugated cardboard, rolled-up newspaper, or hollow bamboo on top of the soil. During the day the earwigs will crawl into the small openings of the traps. Every few days, shake out the traps and dispose of the insects.

Earwig trap

slug trap

A slug-bait trap can be made from a cottage cheese or yogurt container. Make holes in the sides around the bottom of the container. Place commercially available slug bait inside the container and replace the lid securely. Put the trap among the plants and empty the dead slugs as required. This trap keeps the slug bait dry and away from pets.

Biological Control

Biological control is one component of an insect control method known as Integrated Pest Management (IPM). IPM is the combined use of chemical, cultural, biological, and other methods to suppress pest populations to below damaging levels, with minimum side effects. The biological control component uses predatory and parasitic insects, or diseases, to eliminate pest species or reduce their number to below economically damaging levels.

The major drawback of biological control is that some control organisms are not available locally, so you may not be able to get them in time to do much good. Fortunately, biological control and IPM are increasing in importance, and it should become easier to obtain control agents quickly and at a reasonable price. For a more detailed coverage of biological control and IPM, consult the books listed in Appendix D. Sources of biological control agents are provided in Appendix C.

The female Encarsia formosa *laying her egg in a whitefly larva.*

Some biological control agents deserve special mention because they have worked well for the home gardener. *Bacillus thuringiensis*, also called Bt, has proven to be very effective in controlling cabbage worms and the caterpillar stages of many other pests. At least two applications are required. Bt is sold under the trade names of Dipel and Thuricide.

A small wasp called *Encarsia formosa* has been reported by many greenhouse owners to be very effective in controlling whiteflies. The wasp lays its eggs in the whitefly larvae, and when the eggs hatch, the young wasps eat their hosts.

A new product called SEEK is effective in controlling the cabbage root maggot, pillbugs, root weevils, cutworms, and many other soil-dwelling insects.

Commercial Chemical Insecticides

These are usually divided into two categories: botanical insecticides and synthetic insecticides.

Botanical insecticides such as nicotine, pyrethrum, rotenone, ryania, and sabadilla are extracted from plants. Except for nicotine, they are considered less toxic to mammals than synthetic insecticides and break down rapidly into harmless substances. They should nevertheless be used with great care, because you can become very ill if you breathe or eat the insecticide. Botanicals will also kill beneficial insects, so it is best not to use them when practicing biological control methods.

At the Amity gardens we have never used synthetic chemical insecticides, such as Malathion, diazinon, sevin, etc. Our "home remedies" and biological controls have worked well, even if their use has sometimes meant sharing part of the harvest with some insects. To find out more about botanical and synthetic chemical insecticides, contact your extension agent for the most current information and application procedures.

Insect Identification

When you see a bug in your greenhouse, cold frame, or cloche, you need first to decide what kind of insect it is, before you make decisions about control measures. It may turn out to be a beneficial predator you want to keep around to help control pests. A good tool to have is a 10-power magnifying hand lens so you can make closer inspections of plants. Be sure to check under leaves and at the base of the stem in or on the soil, because insects frequently will congregate there.

Aphid-infested

Ants herding aphids

Aphids

DESCRIPTION: Aphids are small (about ⅛ inch long), pear-shaped insects that suck plant juices and excrete honeydew on which a black fungus grows. They feed on almost any plant and can usually be found in colonies on the growing tips, undersides of leaves, and between leaves and stems. They thrive over a wide temperature range and in moderate humidity. Populations can build up rapidly. Ants eat honeydew, so they protect and "herd" aphid populations to ensure their supply.

DAMAGE: Curling leaves, stunted plant growth, yellowing of leaves, death of plant.

CONTROL:
1. Hard water spray.
2. Soap sprays.
3. Home-made repellents.
4. Biological control with lady beetles, lacewings, praying mantises.

Cabbage Root Maggots

DESCRIPTION: The adult (the size of a small housefly) lays eggs near the base of a host plant (primarily the Brassica family), and white maggots burrow into and feed on the root and stem below the soil surface.

DAMAGE: The maggots eat the roots and stem below the soil surface, killing or stunting the plant. Cauliflower, broccoli, and Chinese cabbage are most susceptible to attack.

CONTROL:
1. The peak egg-laying seasons are from mid-April through May and in early fall. Plant before mid-March or after mid-May, so seedlings can get large enough to survive damage.
2. Hot caps over plants prevent the fly from laying eggs.
3. SEEK is an effective biological control agent.

Healthy seedling

Damaged seedling

Cabbageworms

DESCRIPTION: White moth that lays eggs on cabbages and other brassicas. The green caterpillar stage feeds on the plant.

DAMAGE: The caterpillar is a voracious eater, chewing holes in leaves.

CONTROL:

1. Cover young plants with a netting to stop the moth from laying eggs.
2. Pick off the caterpillars by hand.
3. Spray with *Bacillus thuringiensis*.

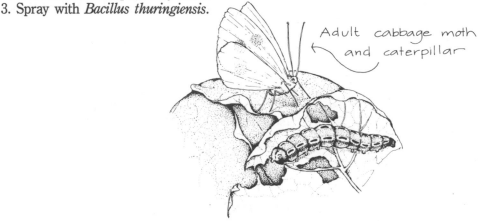

Adult cabbage moth and caterpillar

Flea Beetles

DESCRIPTION: Small, black shiny beetle ($\frac{1}{16}$ to $\frac{1}{8}$ inch long) found chewing leaves of plants.

DAMAGE: Adults chew tiny holes in leaves, giving them a "buckshot" appearance. Flea beetles are particularly attracted to tomatoes, eggplants, peppers, potatoes, and seedlings of all types.

CONTROL:

1. Since flea beetles attack the least vigorous plants, give seedlings good soil and fertilizing conditions.
2. Spray with repellents.
3. Rotate crops regularly.

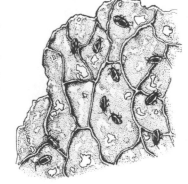

Mealybugs

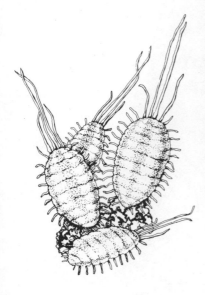

DESCRIPTION: White, cottonylike insects (about ¼ inch long) that crawl slowly over the plant, sucking out the sap and excreting sticky honeydew that attracts molds and ants. Mealybugs can be found on all parts of the plant, but they are typically clustered on stem tips and new growth. Eggs are visible as a cottony mass.

DAMAGE: Wilting, yellowing, and distortion of leaves. Look for patches of sooty mold growing on honeydew that drops underneath infested plants.

CONTROL:
1. Wash with hard water spray or soap spray.
2. Using a Q-tip, touch each mealybug with a dab of alcohol.
3. The Australian lady beetle is a good biological control agent. The green lacewing will also feed on mealybugs, but is not as effective.

Scale

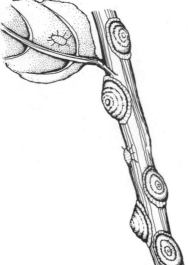

DESCRIPTION: Small (about ¼ inch long), wingless insects with an oval body shape and a waxy or scalelike covering. They can be found on both leaves and stems, and can form thick encrustations. Scale is a common problem on ornamental plants. Eggs hatch into crawlers similar in appearance to mealybugs. This is the best stage for treatment. After finding a suitable feeding site, they settle down and lay down armored scales shaped like oyster shells.

DAMAGE: Scales are sap-sucking insects which cause yellow or brown areas around feeding site.

CONTROL:
1. Remove infested leaves.
2. Insecticidal soap is effective on the crawling stages.
3. A small parasitic wasp, *Aphytis melinus*, lays eggs under the waxy shell of the scale, and the hatched eggs feed on the scale.

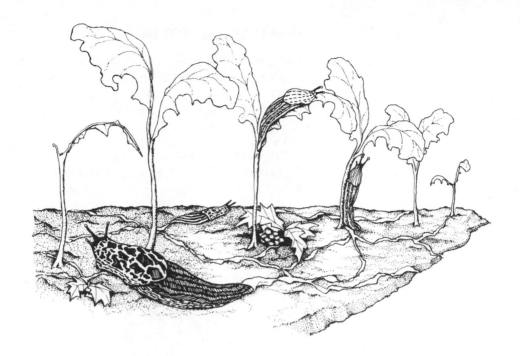

Slugs and Snails

DESCRIPTION: For our purposes, we can say that a slug is a snail without a shell and a snail is a slug with a shell. Both leave a glistening mucous trail. They are attracted to the high humidity in cold frames and cloches and can do a lot of damage, especially at night. Eggs are laid under leaves or debris.

DAMAGE: They will eat plant leaves, roots, and flowers. Vegetable starts can disappear overnight if slugs invade your garden. Slugs are most active in the spring and fall. Dry weather and frosts curtail their activity.

CONTROL:
1. Slugs are night feeders, so make night raids and pick them out of the garden and surrounding area.
2. Set traps with commercial slug bait.
3. Lay out boards and remove slugs which crawl underneath.
4. Slugs don't like to cross diatomaceous earth or wood ash. These can border your beds, but will have to be replaced following rains.

Sow Bugs and Pill Bugs

DESCRIPTION: Gray oval-shaped bugs (¼ to ½ inch long) with armorlike scales. Pill bugs roll into a ball when disturbed, sow bugs run away.

DAMAGE: They feed at night on roots and stems of seedlings.

CONTROL:
1. Trap under boards as for slugs.
2. Diatomaceous earth destroys their soft undersides.
3. SEEK is an effective biological control.

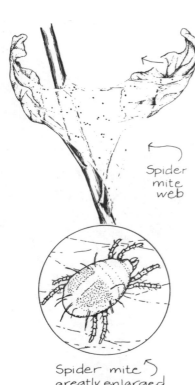

Spider mite web

Spider mite greatly enlarged

Spider Mites

DESCRIPTION: Very small (almost microscopic in size) and oval shaped. If you have a hand lens, look for two dark spots on the back of a yellowish or greenish body. Check for small, whitish cobwebs that they spin between leaves and stems and on the growing tips of plants. Spider mites can be found on a broad range of plants. The potential offspring from one mite would be 13 million during her lifetime. This is one of the most common pest problems encountered in under-cover gardening.

DAMAGE: Spider mites pierce leaves and suck out plant juices, causing pale speckling on the leaves. This will stunt plant growth and eventually kill the plant.

CONTROL:
1. Spider mites do best at high temperatures and low humidity, so mist plants frequently and vent often.
2. A hard water spray.
3. Soap sprays.
4. *Phytoseiulus persimilis*, a predatory mite, feeds on the spider mite.

Spotted Cucumber Beetles

DESCRIPTION: Similar in appearance to lady beetle, but greenish yellow with a small black head and black spots on the back.
DAMAGE: Chews holes in plant leaves. The cucumber beetle prefers bean seedlings but will attack other plants as well. Vigorous plants will survive without an effect on crop yield.
CONTROL:
1. Pick off by hand.

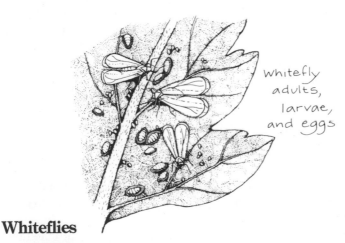

whitefly adults, larvae, and eggs

Whiteflies

DESCRIPTION: Small (1/16 inch long), white moth-like insects that fly when the host plant is disturbed. They attack fewer types of plants than do spider mites, with tomatoes and cucumbers some of their favorite host plants. Whiteflies can usually be found on the underside of the actively growing top leaves. The juvenile stage is a wingless nymph.

DAMAGE: Both adult and nymph suck sap from stems and leaves. Symptoms of damage are weakened plants, yellow mottled leaves, and general discoloration of leaves.
CONTROL:
1. Soap sprays.
2. Sticky traps.
3. A parasitic wasp, *Encarsia formosa*, and the green lacewing, *Chrysopa carnea*, both prey on whiteflies.

Severe whitefly damage

Plant Diseases

The best way to reduce the chance of disease is to follow the management tips outlined at the beginning of this chapter and the sanitation tips in Chapter 7. It is difficult to treat a disease once it has infected your plant. Sometimes you can save a plant by removing just the infected part, but more often you will have to destroy the entire plant or risk spreading the disease to other plants.

Damping-off Disease

DESCRIPTION: A fungal disease that affects the stems and roots of seedlings.
DAMAGE: Causes seedlings to collapse suddenly. Usually the stem right at soil level has rotted.
CONTROL:
1. Use pasteurized soil to prevent initial infection.
2. Plant cannot be revived, but good ventilation and drier soil will prevent the fungus from spreading.
3. Avoid overcrowding and remove sickly seedlings quickly.

Downy Mildew

DESCRIPTION: A white fungus that grows in patches on the undersides of leaves.
DAMAGE: The part of the leaf above the mildew often turns yellow.
CONTROL:
1. Destroy infected leaves.
2. Increase ventilation.
3. Baking soda sprinkled on the fungus controls it.

Gray Mold (Botrytis)

DESCRIPTION: A fungus disease that is encouraged by high humidity. A gray fur can cover fruit, flowers, leaves, and stems.
DAMAGE: Causes the affected area to rot.
CONTROL:
1. Reduce humidity and increase ventilation.
2. Remove infected parts of the plant.
3. Reduce watering.

Powdery Mildew

DESCRIPTION: A fungus that covers leaves and young shoots with a gray or white powder. It has the appearance of powdered sugar dusted on the leaves. Brown patches on leaves with a gray powder beneath are another sign of powdery mildew.
DAMAGE: Destroys affected area.
CONTROL:
1. Destroy infected leaves.
2. Increase ventilation.

Root Rot

DESCRIPTION: A fungus that causes the roots of plants to rot. Dark brown or black patches can often be found at the base of the stem.

DAMAGE: The plant becomes increasingly unhealthy, the lower leaves yellowing and the whole plant wilting easily until it collapses.

CONTROL:

1. Use pasteurized soil to prevent initial infection.
2. Remove any infected plants.
3. Reduce watering.

Tobacco Mosaic and Cucumber Mosaic Viruses

DESCRIPTION: First indicated by mottled or discolored leaves. Aphids and other sucking insects are common carriers of viruses. Tobacco mosaic virus can be transmitted by cigarette smokers.

DAMAGE: Yellow mottled patches on leaves, stunted growth, and distorted leaves.

CONTROL:

1. Once the plant is infected, usually it cannot be saved. Destroy the infected plant.
2. Wash hands and tools to prevent spreading of the disease.
3. Spray plants with skim milk as a preventative for mosaic viruses.

Fusarium and Verticillium Wilts

DESCRIPTION: A fungus that causes leaves to gradually become yellow and wilt, usually old leaves first.

DAMAGE: Yellowing of leaves and wilting of plant.

CONTROL:

1. Use resistant varieties.
2. Use pasteurized soil to prevent initial infection.

Appendixes

Seed Catalogs

*—Carries varieties especially for greenhouses
F—Flowers
H—Herbs
V—Vegetables
T—Tropical Plants

F, H, V   Abundant Life Seed Foundation
P.O. Box 772
Port Townsend, WA 98368

H   Casa Yerba Gardens
Star Route 2, Box 21
Days Creek, OR 97429-9604

T*   Exotica Seeds
25008 E Vista Way, Suite 125
Vista, CA 90046

F, H, V   Good Seed Company
P.O. Box 702
Tonasket, WA 98855

F, H, V   Harris Seeds
Moreton Farm
3670 Buffalo Road
Rochester, NY 14624

V*   Johnny's Selected Seeds
299 Foss Hill Road
Albion, ME 04910

F, H, V, T*   Mellinger's Inc.
2310 W South Range Road
North Lima, OH 44452

V   Mountain Seed and Nursery
P.O. Box 9107
Moscow, ID 83843

H, F, V   Nichols Garden Nursery
1190 N Pacific Highway
Albany, OR 97321

H, V, F*   Stokes Seeds, Inc.
              Box 548
              Buffalo, NY 14240

V   Territorial Seed Company
              P.O. Box 27
              Lorane, OR 97451

V*   Twilley Seeds
              P.O. Box F65
              Trevose, PA 19047

APPENDIX B

Garden and Greenhouse Supplies

1. Check the yellow pages in your area.

2. Brookstone
   127 Vose Farm Road
   Peterborough, NH 03458

3. Charley's Greenhouse Supply
   1569 Memorial
   Mt. Vernon, WA 98273

4. Indoor Garden Supply Inc.
   911 NE 45th Street
   Seattle, WA 98105

5. Indoor Gardening Supplies
   Box 40567H
   Detroit, MI 48240

6. Smith & Hawken Tool Co.
   25 Corte Madera
   Mill Valley, CA 94941

7. Steuber Distributing Co.
   P.O. Box 100
   Snohomish, WA 98290

8. Stupy Greenhouse Division
   120 E 112th Avenue
   North Kansas City, MO 64116

Sources of Beneficial Insects

SM—Predatory mites that attack spider mites
GL—Green lacewing (*Chrysopa carnea*)
PM—Preying mantids (*Tenodera aridiflora*)
WF—Whitefly parasite (*Encarsia formosa*)
MD—Mealybug destroyer (*Crytolaemus montrouzieri*)
FP—Fly parasites
LB—Lady beetles (*Hippodamis convergens*)
AP—Aphid parasite (*Trichogramma* sp.)
RS—Red scale parasite (*Aphytis melinus*)
RM—Cabbage root maggot predator and predator of other soil-dwelling pests
(*Neoplectana* sp.)

SM, WF	Applied Bio-nomics Ltd. Agriculture Canada Research Station 8801 E Saanich Road Sidney, BC, Canada V81 1H3
SM	Biotactics, Inc. 7765 Lakeside Drive Riverside, CA 92509
AP, FP, GL	California Green Lacewings 54 S Bear Creek Merced, CA 95340
AP, FP, GL, LB, RS, MD, SM, WF	Organic Pest Management 19920 Forest Park Drive NE Seattle, WA 98155
RS, WF, FP, GL MD, LB, PM, SM	Peaceful Valley Farm Supply 11173 Peaceful Valley Road Nevada City, CA 95959
GL, LB, AP, RS SM, WF, MD	Rinson-Vitova Insectaries P.O. Box 95 Oak View, CA 93022
RM	Territorial Seed Company P.O. Box 27 Lorane, OR 97451

Selected Gardening References

Cold Frames and Cloches

Aquatias, P. 1978. *Intensive Culture of Vegetables on the French System*. Harrisville, N.H.: Solar Survival Press.

Doscher, P., T. Fisher, and K. Kolb. 1981. *Intensive Gardening Round the Year*. Brattleboro, Vt.: The Stephen Green Press.

Hill, L. 1981. *Successful Cold-Climate Gardening*. Brattleboro, Vt.: The Stephen Greene Press.

Shewell-Cooper, W.E. 1977. *Basic Book of Cloche and Coldframe Gardening*. London: Barrie and Jenkins Ltd.

Siegchrist, C. 1980. *Building and Using Coldframes*. Pownal, Vt.: Garden Way Publishing.

General Gardening

Browse, P.M. 1979. *Plant Propagation*. New York: Simon and Schuster.

Chan, P. 1977. *Better Vegetable Gardens the Chinese Way*. Pownal, Vt.: Garden Way Publishing.

Clark, D. E. (ed.). 1979. *Sunset New Western Garden Book*. Menlo Park: Lane Publishing Company.

Colebrook, B. 1989. *Winter Gardening in the Maritime Northwest*. Seattle: Sasquatch Books.

Farallones Institute. 1979. *The Integral Urban House*. San Francisco: Sierra Club Books.

Free, M. 1979. *Plant Propagation in Pictures*. New York: Doubleday & Company.

Hylton, W.L. (ed.). 1974. *The Rodale Herb Book*. Emmaus, Pa.: Rodale Press.

Jacobs, B.E.M. 1981. *Profitable Herb Growing at Home*. Pownal, Vt.: Garden Way Publishing.

Jeavons, J. 1979. *How to Grow More Vegetables Than You Ever Thought Possible on Less Land Than You Can Imagine*. Berkeley: Ten Speed Press.

Lorenz, O.A., and D.N. Maynard. 1980. *Knott's Handbook for Vegetable Growers*. New York: John Wiley and Sons.

New Alchemy Institute. 1983. *Gardening for All Seasons*. Andover, Mass.: Brick House Publishing Company.

Newcomb, D. 1981. *Growing Vegetables the Big Yield/Small Space Way*. New York: Jeremy P. Tarcher, Inc.

Organic Gardening magazine. 33 E. Minor St., Emmaus, PA 18099 (10 issues/year, $14.97).

Organic Gardening Staff. 1978. *The Encyclopedia of Organic Gardening.* Emmaus, Pa.: Rodale Press.

Raymond, D. 1982. *Joy of Gardening.* Pownal, Vt.: Garden Way Publishing.

Severn, J. 1978. *Growing Vegetables in the Pacific Northwest.* Seattle: Madrona Publishers.

Seymour, J. 1979. *The Self-Sufficient Gardener.* New York: Doubleday & Co.

Solomon, S. 1989. *Growing Vegetables West of the Cascades.* Seattle: Sasquatch Books.

Wallace, D. (ed.). 1980. *Getting the Most from Your Garden.* Emmaus, Pa.: Rodale Press.

Solar Greenhouse Design and Construction

Alward, R., and A. Shapiro. 1980. *Low-Cost Passive Solar Greenhouses.* National Center for Appropriate Technology, P.O. Box 3838, Butte, MT 59702.

Clegg, P., and D. Watkins. 1978. *The Complete Greenhouse Book.* Pownal, Vt.: Garden Way Publishing.

Magee, T. 1979. *A Solar Greenhouse Guide for the Pacific Northwest.* Ecotope Group, 2812 E. Madison, Seattle, WA 98112.

Mazria, E. 1979. *The Passive Solar Energy Book.* Emmaus, Pa.: Rodale Press.

McCullagh, J.C. (ed.). 1978. *The Solar Greenhouse Book.* Emmaus, Pa.: Rodale Press.

Yanda, B., and R. Fisher. 1981. *The Food and Heat Producing Solar Greenhouse.* Sante Fe: John Muir Publications.

Solar Greenhouse Management

Abraham, G., and K. Abraham. 1975. *Organic Gardening Under Glass.* Emmaus, Pa.: Rodale Press.

Beckett, K.A. 1981. *Growing Under Glass.* New York: Simon and Schuster.

Blake, Claire L. 1972. *Greenhouse Gardening for Fun.* New York: Morrow Quill Trade Paperbacks.

Chapel, P. 1980. *The City Greenhouse Book.* Center for Neighborhood Technology, 570 W. Randolph Street, Chicago, IL 60606.

Crockett, J.U. 1978. *Crockett's Indoor Garden.* Boston: Little, Brown and Company.

DeKorne, J.B. 1978. *The Survival Greenhouse.* Culver City: Peace Press, Inc.

Ellwood, C. 1977. *How to Build and Operate Your Greenhouse.* Tucson: HP Books.

Farallones Institute. 1979. *The Integral Urban House.* San Francisco: Sierra Club Books.

Glegg, P., and D. Watkins. 1978. *The Complete Greenhouse Book.* Pownal, Vt.: Garden Way Publishing.

Halpin, A.M. (ed.). 1980. *Rodale's Encyclopedia of Indoor Gardening.* Emmaus, Pa.: Rodale Press.

Klein, M. 1980. *Horticultural Management of Solar Greenhouses in the Northeast.* The Memphremagog Group, P.O. Box 490, Newport, VT 05855.

McCullagh, J.C. (ed.). 1978. *The Solar Greenhouse Book.* Emmaus, Pa.: Rodale Press.

Nearing, H., and S. Nearing. 1977. *Building and Using Our Sun-Heated Greenhouse.* Pownal, Vt.: Garden Way Publishing.

Nelson, P.V. 1985. *Greenhouse Operation and Management.* Old Tappan, N.J.: Reston Publishing Company.

New Alchemy Institute. 1983. *Gardening for All Seasons.* Acton, Mass.: Brick House Publishing Company.

Smith, S. 1982. *The Bountiful Solar Greenhouse.* Santa Fe: John Muir Publications.

Wolfe, D. 1981. *Growing Food in Solar Greenhouses.* New York: Doubleday & Co., Inc.

Pests and Diseases

Carr, A. 1979. *Rodale's Color Handbook of Garden Insects.* Emmaus, Pa.: Rodale Press.

Costello, R.A., D.P. Elliott, and N.V. Tonks. 1984. *Integrated Control of Mites and Whiteflies in Greenhouses.* Publications Office, Ministry of Agriculture and Fisheries, Legislative Buildings, Victoria, British Columbia, Canada V8W 2Z7.

Farallones Institute. 1979. *The Integral Urban House.* San Francisco: Sierra Club Books.

Flint, M.L., and R. Van den Bosch. 1981. *Introduction to Integrated Pest Management.* New York: Plenum Publishing Corp.

Jordan, W.H. 1977. *Windowsill Ecology.* Emmaus, Pa.: Rodale Press.

Klein M., and L. Gilkeson. 1982. *A Guide to the Biological Control of Greenhouse Aphids.* The Memphremagog Group, P.O. Box 490, Newport, VT 05855.

Metcalf, R., D. Fisher, R. Blazier, B. Francis, S. Wesley. 1980. *Integrated Pest Management for the Home and Garden.* Institute for Environmental Studies, University of Illinois, 408 S. Goodwin Ave., Urbana, IL 61801.

Newcomb, D. 1982. *Rx for Your Vegetable Garden.* New York: Jeremy P. Tarcher, Inc.

Philbrick, H., and J. Philbrick. 1974. *The Bug Book, Harmless Insect Controls.* Pownal, Vt.: Garden Way Publishing.

Yepsen, R.B. (ed.). 1976. *Organic Plant Protection.* Emmaus, Pa.: Rodale Press.

Hydroponics

DeKorne, J.B. 1978. *The Survival Greenhouse.* Culver City: Peace Press, Inc.

The New Alchemy Quarterly. The New Alchemy Institute, 237 Hatchville Rd., East Falmouth, MA 02536.

Resh, H.M. 1978. *Hydroponic Food Production.* Santa Barbara: Woodbridge Press.

Williams, T.J. 1978. *How to Build and Use Greenhouses.* San Francisco: Ortho Books.

Aquaculture

Aquaculture Magazine. P.O. Box 2329, Asheville, NC 28802 (Published bimonthly, $15 a year).

Bardach, J.E., J.H. Ryther, and W.O. McLarney. 1972. *Aquaculture: The Farming and Husbandry of Freshwater and Marine Organisms*. New York: John Wiley and Sons.

Bryant, P., K. Jauncey, and T. Atack. 1980. *Backyard Fish Farming*. Prism Press, 2 South Street, Bridport, Dorset, England DT6 3NQ.

New Alchemy Institute. 1983. *Gardening for All Seasons*. Andover Mass.: Brick House Publishing Company.

The New Alchemy Quarterly. The New Alchemy Institute, 237 Hatchville Rd., East Falmouth, MA 02536.

Spotte, S. 1979. *Fish and Invertebrate Culture*. New York: John Wiley and Sons.

Van Gorder, S.D., and D.J. Strange. 1983. *Home Aquaculture: A Guide to Backyard Fish Farming*. Emmaus, Pa.: Rodale Press.

Acknowledgments

Funds for the research and publication of the first edition of *Gardening Under Cover* were provided by the United States Department of Energy Appropriate Technology Small Grants Program. Amity Foundation is grateful for their support.

A special thanks to Raymond Albano, Ed Evans, Caroline Israel, Barbara Kaykas, Peggy Quinn, Neil Safrin, and Kay Stewart, for their help in collecting seemingly endless pages of data and for turning the Amity greenhouse and gardens into something beautiful.

The author would like to thank the Board of Directors and staff of the Amity Foundation for their support and sponsorship throughout the project. The commitment and sacrifices everyone made are immeasurable.

The following Northwest gardeners reviewed drafts of the manuscript: Nancy Benner, Carol Brewster, Binda Colebrook, Fred Gant, Kate Gessert, Gayle and Ogden Kellogg, Mike Maki, Bob Ross, Steve Solomon, and Carl Woestendiek. The author is indebted to the time they took in making critical comments which helped guide this work to its present form.

There is, unfortunately, not enough room to list the many volunteers that worked at the Amity greenhouse and gardens and the hundreds of Northwest under-cover gardeners who generously shared their experiences during the preparation of this publication. It is to all of you that *Gardening Under Cover* is dedicated.

NORTHWEST GARDENING KNOW-HOW
from Sasquatch Books

Our fine regional gardening books are available at bookstores and selected garden centers throughout the Pacific Northwest. If you wish, you may order copies by mail or phone.

WINTER GARDENING IN THE MARITIME NORTHWEST
Cool Season Crops for the Year-Round Gardener
by Binda Colebrook $10.95

GROWING VEGETABLES WEST OF THE CASCADES
Steve Solomon's Complete Guide to Natural Gardening
by Steve Solomon $14.95

TREES OF SEATTLE
The Complete Tree-Finder's Guide to the City's 740 Varieties
by Arthur Lee Jacobson $16.95

THE BORDER IN BLOOM
A Northwest Garden through the Seasons
by Ann Lovejoy $14.95

THE YEAR IN BLOOM
Gardening for All Seasons in the Pacific Northwest
by Ann Lovejoy $11.95

To order by mail: please send us your Visa or Mastercard number or a check for the total price of books you wish to order, plus $1.50 shipping and handling (WA State residents add 8.1% sales tax).

To order by phone: call (206) 441-6202, have your Visa or Mastercard number ready.

Sasquatch Books publishes nonfiction works on a wide range of regional topics including travel, cooking, history, natural history, sports, and public affairs. Please write or call us to request a catalog.

SASQUATCH BOOKS 1931 Second Avenue, Seattle, WA 98101 (206) 441-5555